WONDERS OF MAN

THE PYRAMIDS
AND SPHINX

by Desmond Stewart

and the Editors

of the Newsweek Book Division

NEWSWEEK, New York

NEWSWEEK BOOK DIVISION

JOSEPH L. GARDNER *Editor*

Janet Czarnetzki *Art Director*
Edwin D. Bayrd, Jr. *Associate Editor*
Laurie P. Phillips *Picture Editor*
Eva Galan *Assistant Editor*
Lynne H. Brown *Copy Editor*
Russell Ash *European Correspondent*

ALVIN GARFIN *Publisher*

WONDERS OF MAN

MILTON GENDEL *Consulting Editor*

1st Printing 1971
2nd Printing 1972
3rd Printing 1973
4th Printing 1974
5th Printing 1975
6th Printing 1976
7th Printing 1977

ISBN: Clothbound Edition 0-88225-006-X
ISBN: Deluxe Edition 0-88225-007-8

Library of Congress Catalog Card No. 76-154725
© 1971—Arnoldo Mondadori Editore, S.p.A.
All rights reserved. Printed and bound in Italy.

Contents

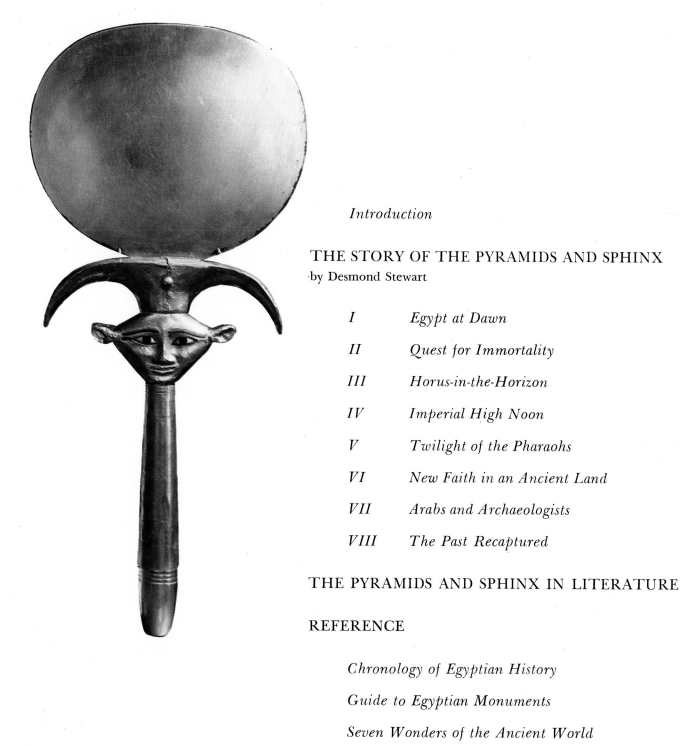

Introduction

Immense, mysterious, almost menacing, the pyramids of Egypt loom on the horizon southwest of modern Cairo. The only survivors of the seven wonders of the ancient world, these awesome tombs have aroused the curiosity and admiration of tourists, scholars, and even those who have lived within their shadow for four and a half millennia. The author of the following narrative uses the pyramids — and their mute, enigmatic sentinel, the Sphinx — as the focal point for a sweeping panorama of Egyptian history.

Out of the mists nearly five thousand years ago appeared the world's first two civilizations — that of Mesopotamia and the splendid edifice of ancient Egypt. With its art, architecture, religion, political organization, and even its cryptic hieroglyphic system of writing, the culture that developed along the Nile took man forward from his prehistoric past in truly giant steps. Their propensity for building monumental tombs in stone has caused the ancient Egyptians to be thought of as a people in love with death, but this was definitely not so. On the contrary, they were so enamored of the life in their fertile valley that they wanted it to last forever — and to prolong life they erected not only the stones of their tombs but also one of history's most complex theologies. Even humble subjects, in time, joined their godly rulers in the quest for immortality.

Ancient Egypt was more than just hulking pyramids, as the numerous illustrations accompanying the text reveal. Delicate papyrus scrolls, vivid frescoes, exquisite jewelry, and portrait statuary of an almost unrivaled realism indicate the breadth of Egyptian creativity — reaching a peak in the illustrious Eighteenth Dynasty, known to us chiefly through the stunning discoveries in King Tutankhamen's tomb.

In the cycle of history, Egypt rose, flourished, declined, and fell. Greeks, Romans, Christians, Arabs — with their own cultures — came to settle in the land of the pharaohs. And until very recently, the glorious past was forgotten, save for outlandishly inaccurate fables and the ever-enduring pyramids. Now, through the genius, patience, and unremitting efforts of several generations of archaeologists, that past can be recaptured and presented here as the fascinating and visually stimulating story that it is.

THE EDITORS

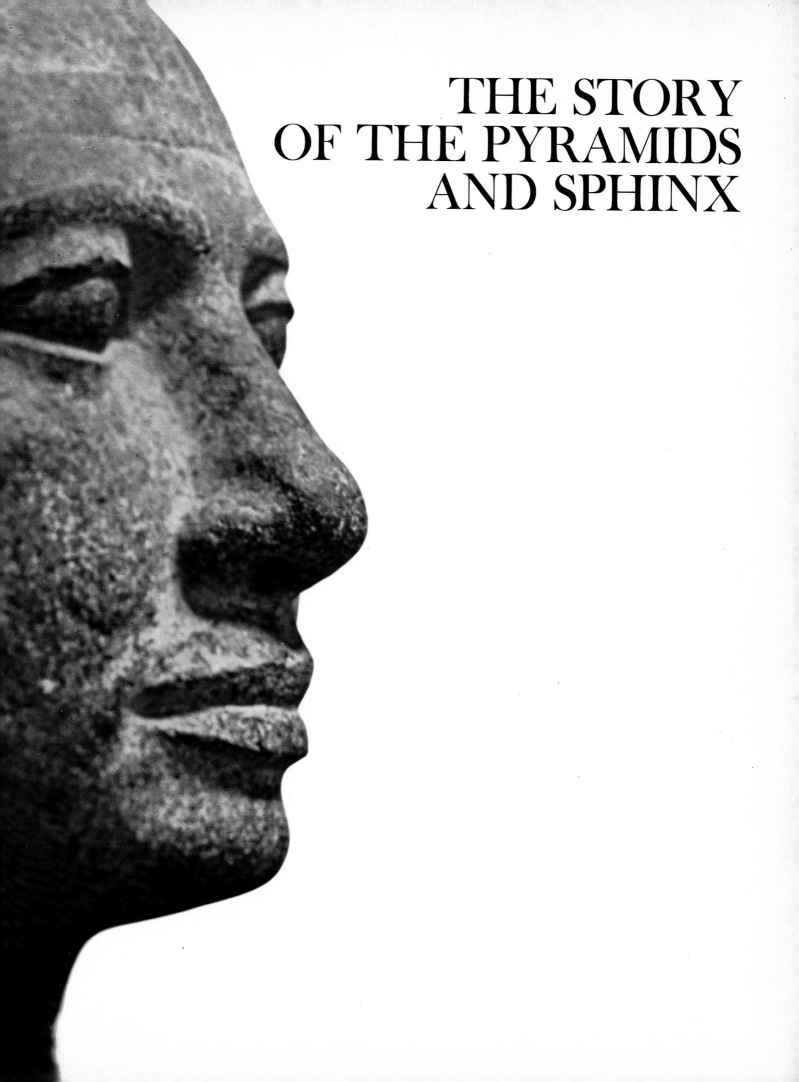

THE STORY
OF THE PYRAMIDS
AND SPHINX

I
Egypt at Dawn

Held apart by a jade-green valley, two ridges of biscuit desert confront each other across the capital of modern Egypt. The western ridge, or plateau of Giza, is the last cliff of the Sahara desert — after the polar regions, the world's least populated zone; the eastern ridge, known to the Egyptians as Mokattam, is the threshold of a narrower wilderness leading to the Red Sea coast. These two ridges were once the quarries — and the western ridge remains the platform — of the planet's oldest, largest, and most enduring monuments of stone.

The three pyramids of Giza are indeed the sole survivors of the seven wonders of the ancient world. How Babylon's gardens hung is as disputed as how the Colossus at the entrance to Rhodes harbor stood; but the Giza pyramids remain so substantial that, when glimpsed from afar, they still seem ideal geometric forms. Only from shouting distance do the ravages wrought by time and its human agents show. The apex of the first and largest pyramid has been blunted by the removal of its capstone and last twelve courses. Only the second pyramid retains, at its apex, some of the original casing of white Mokattam limestone that once made the first two pyramids' slopes as sheer as ice; exposure has turned this fragment desert beige. The red granite that encased the lower part of the smallest pyramid has long since been levered away. Moreover, the rugged, steplike sides of all three pyramids have been gashed by impatient treasure hunters and gouged by quarriers seeking cut stone for palaces and mosques in the city shimmering below. Yet these three monuments are so huge, so resistant to earthquake or human battering, that what has been taken from them no more reduces their essential bulk than a town-destroying avalanche affects an Alp. The eye itself completes the essential line.

In a flatland where the predominant tree is the slender palm, these man-made mountains rule the horizon. They are not alone. South of the village of Abu Roash, directly west of Cairo, more than eighty pyramids survive in greater or lesser repair. But it is the three pyramids of Giza that have always caught the breath of those entering Egypt, from whatever compass point, whether at the heads of armies, like Alexander or Napoleon, or on donkey-back, like the Holy Family in flight from Herod.

Since few travelers land in Egypt without visiting the pyramids, Giza evokes a picnic atmosphere by day. Donkeys, horses, and camels (the two last strangers to the pyramid age) bear newcomers from site to site: tourists from East or West, Soviet technicians, Japanese weighted with optical equipment, Arabs from the Persian Gulf. A swarm of dragomans — their name means "interpreter" and their profession was already thriving when Herodotus, history's father, trudged up to the plateau in the fifth century B.C. — surrounds the pilgrims. One dragoman offers his donkey; another, already in business, focuses an automatic camera while his American client, camel-borne in desert robes, assumes a T. E. Lawrence pose with uplifted whip.

Some yards above the hurly-burly on the sand — and some distance below the original entrance to the Great Pyramid — is the cavelike gash made by a medieval caliph. Climbing to it, you enter the sacred intestines, which once glittered to mirrors of polished bronze or flared to torches but now are lit by electric light. The rough-hewn cave leads to an ascending corridor so low that you trot upward and forward, bending your back,

The only known portrait of Cheops, builder of the Great Pyramid — the world's largest stone structure — is, ironically, this five-inch-high ivory statuette.
   Overleaf:
In the shadow of the three pyramids at Giza that mark the edge of the barren, forbidding desert, farmers plow the lush riverbank of the Nile.

until at last you reach a high processional way leading upward still deeper into the heart of the structure. The Grand Gallery, 153 feet long, is a cathedral aisle without windows or pillars. Its polished limestone walls rise vertically until they are a head higher than the tallest man, then edge inward, three inches at a time, course by course, to form a corbel vault twenty-eight feet above the floor. Higher and higher you tread, conscious that this corbeled roof has withstood the crushing weight of more than two million blocks of stone, averaging two and a half tons, for almost five millennia.

Depending on circumstance, you reach the granite burial chamber of the pyramid builder alone or accompanied. The black walls, the sense of standing at the heart of so much impending stone, imposes solemnity even on the talkative. Man is paltry inside this cool, inert mass that no longer even pretends to serve a master — for the rectangular granite box that the Greeks named a "flesh-eater," or sarcophagus, is tenantless. If you enter the chamber alone — its walls are just over 34 feet from east to west, its ceiling 19 feet, 1 inch above its floor — an eeriness indifferent to life takes hold, a sense of infinity hushing the littleness and brevity of your own concerns. And these, by paradox, suddenly seem of greater value, so that you hurry out, eager for the trees and grasses that symbolize to you — as they did to the builders — the pleasing existence of a human being. As you reach the bottom of the Grand Gallery up which the builder's funeral procession once passed, as you approach the narrow corridor that imposes one-way traffic on all but the slim, you are perhaps delayed by a tidal wave of some sixty Egyptian schoolboys on a day trip with bundles of cakes and

flasks of water. One of the boys is in tears at the awesome dark, and you find that you are glad to be reminded of the thrust of life. Outside in the bright sun you welcome the peddlers and the pestering guides. You are an astronaut from inner space.

If you return at night — and those who have the time return, just as those who have once drunk the Nile drink it again — you wait until *Son et Lumière* and its recorded banalities have been switched off. The huge stars of Egypt take over from the arc lights, heirs of the magnesium flares that lit the Great Pyramid for the Empress of France a century ago. All is velvet dark. In their stables at the foot of the plateau the horses and camels softly champ. A faint flute eddies, or a monotonous love song wafts from Radio Cairo. Up on the plateau, even in summer, a wind stirs — what the Coptic monks who inhabit the desert call the voice of eternity. Now everything festal has gone. No one pesters you as you walk toward the Great Pyramid. Its sides mount until they vanish at some invisible point under the stars. They seem what they were perhaps planned to be, a ladder to heaven. In the absence of the aristocratic casings, the giant blocks hewn from the Giza plateau that were the pyramid's proletarian core are now exposed. But even they, although never intended to be seen, were precisely cut and so closely fitted that a sheet of thinnest paper could not be inserted between one giant granite cube and its neighbor.

You leave the Great Pyramid and approach the second. It is sharper in its angle of ascent and ten feet shorter in overall height; it was made by the son of the builder of the first, and so defers. And then suddenly, hardly expecting it, you see below a shape, a shadow.

Piercing the limestone core of Cheops's pyramid, the narrow passageway of the Grand Gallery retains its aura of mystery despite the installation of electricity.

It solidifies. Your eyes give it a pattern and you remember: the Sphinx! And as you catch the profile of this great face — half-barbaric and half-wiser than ourselves — you feel, if you have never felt it before, a sacred awe. Stone shaped five thousand years before you were born once more effects its spell.

The Egypt dominated by the pyramids is a land of contrasts. You can stand with one leg ankle-deep in clover, the other scuffing driest sand. The pyramids of Giza mark this abrupt edge between the desert and the sown. More significantly, they stand near the frontier between prehistory and history, between a time when men's thoughts, for being unwritten, vanished with the wind and a time when men could transmit their thoughts to the future as well as to their contemporaries — a time symbolized as much by the scribe as by the king. The pyramids are thus more than mere wonders. They are triumphal monuments to a momentous revolution in human history: the decisive changeover from the five thousand centuries in which men were nomads to our relatively brief experience of growing food in settled communities.

Accidents of geography and climate made Egypt uniquely propitious for these first attempts at civilization. The valley through which the Nile pours from south to north — a long terraced gash first in sandstone, then limestone hills — was fashioned long before recorded history by heavings and reheavings of the earth's crust, by deeper and deeper scourings as the upland floods of Ethiopia worked their way north to the Mediterranean Sea. The flooding waters carried with them a silt ideal for agriculture, and that silt created another duality for a country in which dualism seemed

an aspect of life. Originally a great gulf thrust inland from the Mediterranean; the two escarpments of Giza and Mokattam overlooked it as cliffs. Over many millennia the silt slowly filled this gulf, thereby creating a huge fan-shaped wedge of fertile land pushing ever farther north into the sea. Long after it was tamed and heavily settled, the Greeks would name this northern plain, watered by seven branches of the Nile, the Delta, since its shape resembled the triangular fourth letter of their alphabet.

Valley and delta gave the country two distinct regions: Upper (or southern) Egypt, extending south from Giza to the first cataract at Aswan, and Lower (or northern) Egypt, fanning out from the neck between Giza and Mokattam to reach the sea. Both regions benefited from further accidents. The Ethiopian floods, being linked to the monsoon rains of the Indian Ocean, poured down in summer and made the Nile flood at the driest season. The Egyptian new year began around July 19, as the rising of Sirius, the Dog Star, marked the moment when the river normally began to rise. The Nile was not only a source of water; it was a smooth highway easily navigable in both directions. To voyage north from Aswan, you drifted with the river; to return, you hoisted a sail and let the dominant north wind propel you south against the stream.

No other region on earth enjoyed so many blessings. The alluvial soil between the Tigris and Euphrates — known to the Greeks as Mesopotamia and to the Arabs as Iraq — was as rich: it could return an eighty-fold yield for the sown grain. But its two rivers were less kindly than the Nile. As the snow melted in the highlands of what are now Turkey and Iran, the rivers thundered south across a landscape already drenched from winter rains. When water was needed in summer they sulked low between their banks.

Egypt's uniquely convenient valley was uniquely protected against attack. To the north the sea presented a severe obstacle to Neolithic or Bronze Age sailors. To the south the great granite boulders that formed the cataracts blocked the way to boat-borne invaders from what is now Sudan. The Sahara to the west not only barred the way to invaders, but starved them; as a result, the chain of oases running parallel to the Nile was sparsely peopled. Only to the northeast was there an opening toward potentially dangerous, populated regions. If the coastal road through northern Sinai to Palestine provided the thoroughfare by which most of Egypt's future conquerors would come, the same road facilitated expansion when Egypt was strong. It was also a link with other areas of early civilization, in particular Mesopotamia. Thanks to it, the technological and artistic impulses of Sumer and Babylon were felt in Egypt, first in some of the artistic motifs of prehistoric times, and then in architectural forms derived from the brick temples of the Euphrates valley.

The developments in this favored land during the thousand or more years before the pyramid age represent a series of creative advances unrivaled in human experience. But the men who made those first advances could not write and did not build in stone. As a result the fourth millennium before Christ is like some talented, unnamed ancestor in a family tree whose genes send valuable but unacknowledged donations to descendants now alive. Trying to look at prepyramidal Egypt is like trying to get prints from an amateur's

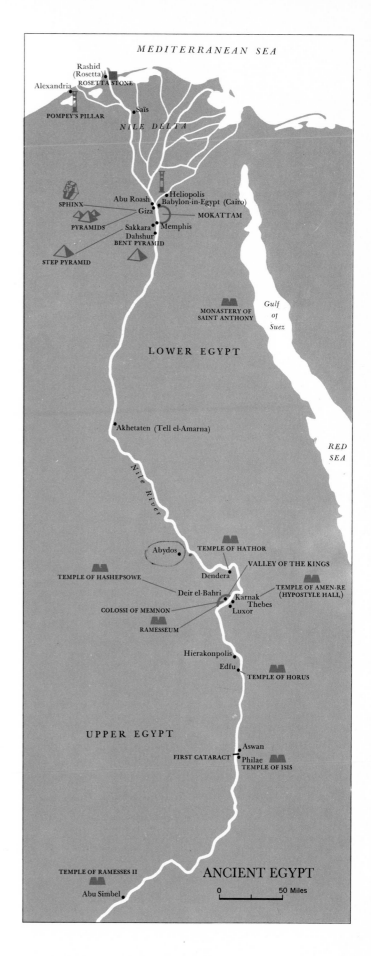

film of an outstanding event. The frames may be out of focus and wrongly exposed, but they are all we have. We are handicapped by the very forces that encouraged the burgeoning of agricultural life — the generous Nile and its damp, rich silt. For while the valley tempted men from the dry, torrid uplands (in those days the Sahara was greener and the valley more jungly than today), it destroyed rather than preserved their traces. Paltry accidents give us glimpses. An untidy grave that happens to be in dry sand, not in engulfing mud, can show us that even in prehistory men were concerned with the hereafter, burying jars of food with the departed. These ancients made no attempt at mummification; instead, the bodies were partially burned and then dismembered before burial.

Prepyramidal men hunted the escarpments for flints, which they worked to razor-sharpness, and those primitive tools litter their excavated camps. Even then men and women were interested in making themselves attractive, and at such sites archaeologists have found slate palettes on which malachite, a copper ore, has been pounded into green eye-paint. Some of these palettes are incised with shorthand vignettes of human prehistory: the investment of villages, the hunting of such wild animals as the lion, giraffe, and hippopotamus — fauna now found much farther to the south, where Uganda adjoins the Sudan.

What we can infer from untidy graves and abandoned flint tools, from mace heads and statuettes, is an accelerating growth of village communities all along the Nile and its delta branches. The men who peopled them were "African," related to their Libyan neighbors to the west and the Nubians to the south. These small communities are the remote ancestors of our modern towns. Discoveries made in them lead directly to our own existence. The taming of wild asses, for example, enabled men to travel farther in less time; the donkey is thus the distant ancestor of the motor car. The training of oxen to pull a plow or a sled was the first step in a serial process toward every machine that has since increased man's power and comfort. The essential thing was that man had escaped dependence on his muscles.

But the most distinctive revolution in this age of tamed animals and improved flint tools had to do with food, the *sine qua non* of human existence. Men had previously gathered berries at random or shot into the wandering herds. These early nomads must have had moments of happiness or content. They possessed, in personal freedom, one great good that civilization would often menace. But this theoretical good was bought at the practical price of frequent dearth and early death. If the nomads — or Bedouins, as they are still called by the Arabs — enjoyed their freedom, they enjoyed it briefly and in small numbers. They could never expect to amass or store a surplus. Thus they had no protection against a time of scarcity and no provision for the time when they would be old. Though they had an abundance of land to roam across, and war — as distinct from raids or clashes — was unknown, this was largely because they had little to guard or steal.

Food growing became possible after the discovery that certain grasses, when carefully tended on the right soil, could yield a manifold crop of edible grains. Certain trees, such as the date palm, could give an accumulable surplus of fruit. Patches planted with corn, orchards of slow-maturing fruit trees, tied men to a

territory. Villages with something to value had something to guard, something that would be coveted by less successful villagers or the men who still lived as nomads. Generalized anxiety became a probable by-product of the movement from food-gathering to a food-growing economy, and that anxiety was not confined to defense. Fertility seemed the supreme good — in animals, crops, and man himself; sterility seemed the final curse. For whereas a hunting pack was not the more effective for being large, a village needed many hands to dig and maintain the canals, as well as for other communal tasks, including defense.

Fertility could be stimulated by magic processes. Magic sprang from the sense that nature was one sympathetic whole, that the names of things conferred power over the things themselves and that verbal formulae or acted rituals could work man's will over nature. Many villages had a patron animal, or symbol; that animal did not stand for itself but for an aspect of the power behind fertility. Such symbols differed one from another, but they had a common ground in concern for offspring and a good harvest; they were vitalized by the certainty that the universe was ruled by forces that man must control or placate. They derived from a situation in which men, newly descended into the valley, had begun to control the river — first through the clearing of a small patch by the bank; then, with expanding ambition, through the clearing of whole swamps, driving back marauding creatures and planting the cleared ground with grain, which the hooves of domesticated animals such as pigs and sheep would tread into the flood-time mulch.

The problems of defense were more prosaic. Who-

ever could command the best weapons could control a village or a group of villages; in return he could offer them security against attack. The discovery (almost certainly in western Asia) that certain stones, when heated, produced a metal that could be cast in molds and sharpened into knives gave more power to those who had them. For while a flint knife was sharp, it broke easily and was then useless. A bronze instrument could be remolded and resharpened almost indefinitely. Instruments of bronze were for the few. Copper was relatively rare, and its alloy tin, rare indeed. The commander of a small force of men armed with bronze could dominate a host of villagers armed with flints.

In this blurred film of inference and guesswork, of peoples of uncertain origin and mummies without names, one frame suddenly clarifies with exquisite sharpness. It is the record of a named individual and a profoundly significant historic action.

A large slate palette, discovered just north of Edfu and now housed in Cairo Museum, monumentalizes the union of Egypt. This event was considered by the Egyptians as the initial point in human history, and it has as much right as any event to this preeminence. Certainly it was the event that unstoppered an unrivaled outflow of human energy; it marks the beginning of a process that culminated in the pyramids of Giza. It was an event that passed, two thousand years after it happened, into the patter of dragomans who retailed it to the inquisitive Greeks, the first European visitors to Egypt. "The priests," Herodotus wrote, "said that Menes was the first king of Egypt, and that it was he who raised the dyke which protects Memphis from the inundations of the Nile."

The scenes carved in a low relief on both sides of the votive palette at left commemorate the most momentous event in Egyptian history: the unification of Upper (southern) and Lower (northern) Egypt by Narmer, a tribal chieftain from the south. A First Dynasty stele (right) unearthed at Abydos in the tomb of King Zet is dominated by the figure of Horus, the falcon-god of the north whose association with royalty had been established by Narmer. Horus is perched atop a serekh, *or frame, that represents the royal palace, within which is poised the hieroglyph for Zet's name, a serpent.*

At the top of both sides of this palette the king's name is shown by two small pictures, one of the *n'r* fish, the other of the *mr* chisel. This spells "Narmer" on the same principle employed in the game of charades, where a symbol or action is found for each syllable of a secretly chosen word and the players must guess the total meaning. It is as if we wrote "Washington" by juxtaposing pictures of a laundress and a tun of beer, or "Roosevelt" by balancing a flower against a representation of the African veldt.

Egyptologists have attempted to explain the conflict between the Menes of Greek legend (who appears as Meni at the head of a list of kings in an Egyptian temple) and Narmer by the fact that all Egyptian kings had five names, including a prenomen and a nomen. Narmer is thought to be another name for Menes.

The palette does much more than simply give another name to a king whom we already knew through legend. Both of its sides illustrate the circumstances of the unification of Egypt through pictures in low relief that combine primitive strength with an already sophisticated skill. On one side the king, wearing the tall conical crown of Upper Egypt, holds with one hand the forelock of a humiliated enemy while his other hand brandishes the mace with which he will brain his captive. To the right, a peremptory hawk stands dominant over a cushion-shaped lump prowed with a human head and exuding six papyrus plants. In his *Egyptian Grammar,* Sir Alan Gardiner expounded the meaning of this symbol-sentence as: "The falcon-god Horus [i.e., the king] leads captive the inhabitants of the papyrus-land [i.e., Lower Egypt]."

On the reverse side the palette shows the king wear-ing the more complex, tufted crown of Lower Egypt. He stands, twice the size of his allies, three times the size of his standard-bearers, before ten enemies stacked like two piles of cordwood, their cut heads neatly placed between their legs. These images suggest that the union of Egypt was accomplished by an act of war; the picture of a ship implies that Narmer sailed to the scene of his victory. Lower down, however, a note of reconciliation is struck. A pair of feline monsters compose, with their intertwining, giraffe-like necks, a circle wherein eye-paint could be mixed. They demonstrate that the king had achieved a union of equals. This union was later symbolized by a double crown, which combined the two older crowns in one.

If the union of Egypt had represented the simple triumph of south over north, it would hardly have remained a poised duality. But the very symbols of the palette conceal a double victory: the probable physical victory of the south had been preceded by an earlier nonmilitary victory of the north. This hidden, spiritual victory is implied in the symbol of Narmer's kingship, the falcon-god of the north, Horus. An Egyptian genius for visual metaphor easily equated the highest flying bird in Egypt with Re, the sun. The falcon remained the essential symbol of Egyptian kingship throughout thirty ancient dynasties — even the Roman emperors, in their role as rulers of Egypt, were shown as hawks. The prenomen every king bore was his "Horus name."

Horus, the son of Osiris by his sister Isis, features in a myth so fundamental to Egyptian thought that it can hardly be omitted from any first chapter on Egyptian history. The myth was so popular that in later versions a basic Cain-and-Abel struggle became entangled in a

jungle of detail. The bare bones of the myth tell of a beneficent king, Osiris, who rescues men from cannibalism by teaching them how to grow corn and cultivate the vine. Osiris has a jealous brother Seth, who beguiles the trusting Osiris into a trick coffin and then kills him, throwing his brother's body into the Nile. The kindly river-god carries the corpse as far as Byblos, the port in Lebanon from which the Egyptians, like King Solomon after them, imported timber for palaces and temples. Isis follows her husband-brother and finds his coffin clasped in the branches of a tree in the king's palace. She brings it back to Egypt, only to have Seth discover it and cut the dead king into fourteen pieces. Isis then traces each portion and gives it burial, marking each grave with a shrine. More remarkable, the dead Osiris, revived by magic, begets upon her body a son, whom she brings up to avenge his father. This son, Horus, eventually wrests Egypt from the animal-god Seth and puts it under Re.

Like all Egyptian myths, this story can be understood on several levels. Osiris with his pale green face is a god of vegetation and as such a symbol of fertility and resurrection. Known from earliest times as "the god at the head of the stair," Osiris rules the afterworld and controls its mechanisms of judgment and salvation. The details of his posthumous dismemberment probably refer to predynastic methods of burial. But to those interested in Egyptian origins the myth embodies one detail of overriding interest. Seth was the animal-god of Ombos, a town in Upper Egypt. The triumph of Horus over Seth thus represents the triumph of a northern over a southern cult. Horus therefore may stand for a prehistoric happening: the entry

into Egypt of more advanced religious ideas brought by men affected, in all probability, by Mesopotamian culture. That there was some such influence from Asia is evident in the Egyptian language itself, which represents a fusion of Hamitic (Mesopotamian) roots and Semitic grammatical forms.

The triumph of Horus did not involve the banishment of Seth from the Egyptian pantheon. With a tolerance baffling to the logically minded, the Egyptians allowed him to exist in equilibrium with his resurrected victim and his victim's victorious son — some rulers of Egypt even took Seth's name. All rulers in some sense embodied Seth along with Horus, and their wives commonly bore the title "She-Who-Sees-Horus-and-Seth." Just as, in the profoundest religious texts, spells against snakes and scorpions balanced passages that foreshadow the Hebrew psalms, Seth remained. (Significantly, the dynasty that would do him greatest honor would be the alien Hyksos, whose expulsion marks one of the great rebirths in Egypt's history.) The Egypt united by a king from the south was permanently tied to a religious tradition derived from the north.

The Narmer palette thus proclaims that Egypt was a poised duality from the beginning and that it began with a bang. The bang's date is still uncertain, but it no longer sways between such wide dates as was the case fifty years ago; most Egyptologists now ascribe the unification of Egypt to within 150 years of 3100 B.C. Under two archaic dynasties (conjecturally dating from around 3100 to 2700 B.C.) and the four succeeding dynasties of the Old Kingdom, basic patterns in religion, law, language, and hieroglyphic writing were incised that would endure in a recognizable unity for three thousand years. Modes of artistic representation that were later regarded as sacred norms were at this time innovations vigorously fresh.

The Egyptians' first collective discovery had been that strength was derived from unity and was the precondition of success. The king did not merely symbolize strength; he embodied it as the fount of justice and authority, as the man who made decisions and saw that they were obeyed. Later spectators of what these kings achieved assumed that they must have been hated tyrants; the tales of dragomans encouraged such beliefs. But the men whose labors these kings had organized may have seen things otherwise. They recognized that anarchy and disorder threatened a life that had begun to provide moments of pleasure even for serf-like peasants bent over the fields; draftboards and musical instruments survive to tell their unmilitary tale. It was certainly not the last time that a society willingly surrendered some freedom in return for greatly increased security.

The freedom possible in a primitive Bedouin or a modern Scandinavian society was hardly possible in a land with no long tradition of settled life but dependent for its food on irrigation. Years of low Nile have brought famine throughout Egyptian history. They drove home the lesson that lack of water, through some men's failing to maintain canals or through other men's taking more than their share, could quickly empty a granary or destroy an orchard. Egypt discovered a truth particularly applicable to societies that depend on the control of a great river: a central authority able to maintain the canals and to apportion their water is a good, not a bad thing. (This truth was

to be exemplified in the later history of Mesopotamia, a rich country when properly maintained but a near-desert when its canal system fell into decay.) As collective man crossed the threshold of the agricultural revolution he recognized certain harsh truths that Thomas Hobbes was to enunciate to men on the brink of the industrial revolution:

> The final cause, end or design of men (who naturally love Liberty, and Dominion over others,) in the introduction of that restraint upon themselves (in which we see them live in Commonwealths,) is the foresight of their own preservation and of a more contented life thereby; that is to say, of getting themselves out from that miserable condition of War, which is necessarily consequent . . . to the natural passions of men, when there is no visible Power to keep them in awe, and tie them by fear of punishment to the performance of their Covenants.

The flail, a symbol of the power to punish, was, with the shepherd's crook, a symbol of kingship throughout ancient Egyptian history.

Menes-Narmer not only united valley and delta but indirectly gave the new nation a durable name. The great new capital that he built at the apex of the delta, known to the Greeks as Memphis, was known to his subjects as Hutkaptah, the Place of the *Ka* (or spiritual double) of Ptah, the chief Memphite god. Hutkaptah was roughly transliterated by the Greeks as Aigyptos, from which our word Egypt derives.

Ptah's temple dominated Memphis; his theologians may have worked out the first of many Egyptian attempts to tidy up the muddle sponsored by the con-servative Egyptian mind, which amiably accepted the coexistence of contradictions and the survival (as we have seen in the case of Seth) of ancient forms alongside the new. Each district tended to exalt its own god, arguing that he incorporated the others as well. As a result Egyptian religion often seems a chaotic polytheism of weird animals and legendary beings. But in the words of a French Egyptologist, the religion was more a monotheism with facets. To the simple-minded, the facets, or totems, were doubtless enough; but the caste of priests who daily fed and clothed the statues of the gods produced a number of inquisitive minds who sought for the divine diamond behind the glinting facets. This diamond would assume many names in Egyptian history and the first may well have been Ptah.

An ancient text records what may be called the Memphite theology. According to a first-millennium version of an archaic text, Ptah was "he who standeth on the earth and toucheth the sky with his head; he whose upper half is the sky and whose lower half is the underworld." Ptah was the reality that flashed in the sun and in the sun-soaring swiftness of the hawk, whose tenderness showed in the gentle eyes of the cow, whose flaming wrath was revealed in the lioness of war. This primal force, by whose fiat gods and men emerged, was usually represented as a bearded, bare-headed man whose lower limbs were tightly swathed in the white garments of a mummy. Ptah's complexion was depicted as palest yellow. This could have been intended to signify the god's intellectual, reflective character. Tied to the soil as they have always been, Egyptians tend to envy those who live an indoor life and to value a protected pallor. The activities with which Ptah was

Worshiped as a god for centuries after his death, Imhotep, the architect of Zoser's tradition-breaking tomb — the Step Pyramid at Sakkara (right) — was also recognized as a man of genius in his own time. The frieze at left once encircled the base of a statue of Zoser.

identified — the working of metals and the administration of justice — were essentially indoor. Another explanation is possible, however, for yellow was also the color employed by Egyptian artists to identify foreigners. The pale complexion of the artificer-god could thus be a recognition that Egypt owed the discovery of metallurgy to non-Egyptians.

Under an administration far ahead of its contemporaries, the Egyptian kingdom expanded dramatically. Narmer's successors created the social infrastructure for the pyramid age.

But the first two dynasties — generally known as the archaic period — form only the forecourt of history. The palette of Narmer and other surviving palettes and temple frescoes that contain the names of early kings fill in no personal details. We do not know whence these kings derived, whether they were native Egyptians or invaders from abroad. It remains a mystery how they established themselves not only as rulers, but as living gods. Archaic Egypt lasted from around 3100 to 2700 B.C., or roughly as long as the Roman Empire in the west. In this crucible many elements melted down to form the Egypt — speaking a language blending Hamitic and Semitic elements, writing it in hieroglyphics — that was to erupt on the horizon with the pyramids of the Old Kingdom. For us, it remains a time of guesswork.

Our next flash of clarity comes with a king whose name in the temple lists was inked in red to show his importance. Zoser, first ruler of the Third Dynasty, deserves red ink on several scores. He was the first ruler anywhere to employ an architect of such individual genius that his name, Imhotep, has survived until the present. Imhotep, at Zoser's bidding, was to build, on the Sakkara ridge above Memphis, the first large-scale edifice in stone that the planet had ever seen. In its ruins a seated statue of Zoser has survived. Though the eyes have been gouged out by thieves, the statue retains an aura of majesty, a living kinship to the Ancient of Days. Imhotep's stone building, six diminishing squares placed on top of each other, is the first recognizable member of the family of tombs that are known as the pyramids.

In the space of less than a century one of Zoser's descendants, Queen Hetep-Heres, would marry Snofru, founder of the Fourth Dynasty and builder of two pyramids, one with sheer, unbroken sides. His two pyramids at Dahshur are the logical developments from Imhotep's Step Pyramid at Sakkara. They are also the immediate forerunner of the Great Pyramid of Giza, built by Snofru's son around 2600 B.C. Snofru's heir, known for more than two thousand years as Cheops, was long swaddled in myths that made him seem as legendary as Menes. Then, in the nineteenth century, in a loft above the burial chamber roof, excavators working on the Great Pyramid discovered a workman's hieroglyph on a block of stone that recorded, without honorific titles, the Egyptian form of Cheops: Khufwey. Cheops was proved to be no less historical than Julius Caesar.

II
Quest for Immortality

We owe the outburst of Egyptian civilization to a series of effective kings; we owe most of what we know of it to the tombs of these same kings. The pyramids and the lion-shaped sphinx that guards them are the visible tips of a society whose secular buildings — the cool, flimsy palaces where the king acted as judge, ordered expeditions to bring granite from Aswan or slaves from Nubia, ate, played draughts, listened to music, and made love — are like the hidden portions of an iceberg, submerged beyond recall in time and sediment. The world ruled by the sun-god Re is buried in the valley. The realm of death, associated with the western desert (beyond which the sun sank every evening), was under the sway of Osiris, father of Horus. His realm has left us more objects, great and small, than any other civilization of the past.

The profusion of Egyptian tombs and the wealth of their contents make it easy to picture the tomb builders as a nation in love with death; throughout the ages mystagogues, necromancers, and false prophets have invoked the ancient Egyptians as their patrons. But what we know of them proves this picture inaccurate. In fact, they so loved the life that could be lived in their delectable valley that they wanted it to last forever. Their success at solving other problems, at keeping their enemies at bay, fostered a metaphysical self-confidence breathtaking in its audacity. They had tamed the ass to carry packs, and oxen to draw sleds and plows; their chisels had forced mountains to yield cut stone; their mattocks had begun to tame the banks of the Nile; their spells could even tame death.

This confidence took two different but related forms in the Egyptians' long history. During the pyramid age they believed that the king, who had been Horus in his lifetime, became Osiris after it; in some way they partook of the immortality of their king. A millennium later, during the New Kingdom, Egyptian confidence advanced to a yet more ambitious plateau: every dead man became identified with Osiris, and so became an immortal god.

There was nothing democratic about the relationship between ruled and ruler in the Old Kingdom. No other society in recorded history has so exalted its monarch. In life he was as far above ordinary mortals as the hawk that was his symbol. Palettes from predynastic times show these rulers to be pugnacious individuals, good at hunting and war. Throughout thirty dynasties and three thousand years the king would be depicted as in command, yet he was not a tyrant. As an incarnate deity he upheld the fundamental order of the universe. His practical and spiritual power merited awe, homage, and tribute. The taxes paid in kind to the royal palace were tributes to a living god upon whose presence and vitality the crops themselves depended. Since the king was part of nature, he would naturally die; but like the dying crops or the setting sun, he would be born again and everything could be reborn with him. According to French Egyptologist Alexandre Moret, a duty was thus imposed on ordinary men: "It was necessary, and it was enough, that they help the gods to support even the test of daily, or periodic, death, and that they contribute, with all their efforts, to make them be reborn." The dead king was reborn as Osiris while a new Horus reigned on earth.

It is probable that in very early times a king who

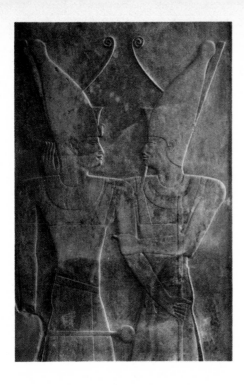

A series of carved pillars from a small temple at Karnak built by Sesostris I to celebrate his hebsed, *or thirtieth reign-year, depict the pharaoh in the embrace of various gods. In this example, Sesostris appears as himself and as Osiris, god of the dead.*

had reigned for thirty years was put to death and so was forced by his subjects into his new Osiris role. In historical times a king who had completed thirty years of rule celebrated a jubilee, or *hebsed,* in which he symbolically became Osiris while still alive. That ceremony, which included a reenactment of the ruler's coronation and a ritual run attesting his agility, helped him to revive his vital force — just as Osiris himself had been revived by the magic of Isis. These jubilees were often repeated at three-year intervals during the remainder of a monarch's reign. But however long preserved, the king's breath would fail at last. He would then take his place in the underworld, where even the sun-god spent half his time.

The prehistoric Egyptians may have believed in a bodily resurrection, but this notion was discarded early in dynastic times. Evidence of that shift can be found in the compilation of religious writings known as the *Book of the Dead* (which will be discussed in detail in Chapter IV). The earliest version is inscribed on a pyramid built by Unas, ninth and last king of the Fifth Dynasty. "Re receives you," the king is told, "soul in heaven, body in earth." This remained the general view for three thousand years. A text dating from a much later period repeats the message: "Your soul is in heaven before Re; your double has what should be given to it with the gods; your spiritual body is glorious among the spirits of fire; and your material body is established in the grave."

The king in the grave remained a power in his own right. He thus differed from the hero of Greek history, whose memory deserved remembrance for his deeds. And he differed dramatically from the ancestors honored in other monarchies because of those forebears' blood connection with the living ruler. The king had become a god of the underworld who could affect life here and now. And since the underworld was the other half of a single, static reality, the dead king would, in that mirror world, have attributes and needs similar to those of the living. Just as he had developed a living form on earth, so there he would develop a spiritual form; just as his personality had grown in his living flesh, so his *ka,* or spiritual double, continued to develop in his corpse.

This process would take time, and the body needed to be preserved carefully from disturbance and decay. Just as the king had enjoyed moving out of his palace when the Egyptian day heat turned abruptly to evening coolness, so the *ka* would wish to do likewise. Just as the king had been fed with the choicest food and refreshed with beer as well as wine, so the *ka* would need equivalents. Just as the monarch had used a fleet of boats to go sailing from the Memphis wharf, so his spiritual double would need ships in the hereafter. Just as he had been waited on here, so he would need servants there. Just as he had been surrounded by a court, so his tomb would dwarf a dormitory town of smaller tombs wherein his advisers would sleep within call.

In life, the kings had no need for substantial buildings or solid luxury. Palaces of mud-brick, linen robes, and wooden beds sufficed for a living Horus in the gentle, almost rainless climate. Reigns varied in length from a few days to the sixty-six years of Ramesses II. Eternity lasted infinitely longer than the longest mortal life, and a house for eternity — as Egyptians called the tomb — had to be far more durable than a palace. That

This painted limestone bas-relief from the Old Kingdom mastaba, or rectangular stone tomb, of a high official named Ptah-hotep portrays the deceased at his funerary feast. Seated on a stool before a richly laden offering table, Ptah-hotep accepts the gifts of wine and food borne by his servants. In the narrow horizontal registers above his head are carved rows of birds and animals representing the abundance that will sustain his ka, or soul, in the afterlife.

it would cost much labor and stone to make it durable did not seem to matter. The royal tomb was not the preserve of an egoist displaying his wealth, nor a municipal monument; it was a place of immense importance to society. Its purpose, inside the framework of Egyptian assumptions, was as functional as that of a power station, and it was contrived with as practical ends in mind. The tomb was the place in which the dead king, securely buried, could receive homage and nourishment; from it the king could make his successful journey to the afterworld and thence radiate blessings back to his people.

The tomb's first function was therefore to act as a safe-deposit vault for a gold-lapped, gift-surrounded body — and this demanded security such as later civilizations would contrive for banks. The tomb's second function was as the focus for a religious cult — and this required that it be as conspicuous and imposing as the places of pilgrimage and prayer in other religions. In short, an Old Kingdom tomb had to combine the functions of a great cathedral and Fort Knox. In the long run the two functions were irreconcilable. For a dead body to be secure, it needed secrecy, not advertisement. Significantly, the one Egyptian king whose body and treasures did survive almost intact to our own time was interred in an obscure corner of a hidden valley. The astonishing superstructures of the great tombs were like beckoning fingers to those ready to risk the hereafter and its possible pains for present gain — and every Egyptian generation would produce its quota of such sacrilegious thieves. But though the tomb builders rarely managed to outwit the persistent thief, they did succeed in constructing monuments whose grandeur impresses us to this day. In other responses to their funerary needs they would create works of art whose durability depends not on millions of tons of stone but on beauty's imperishable power.

To take the second first: art developed rapidly after the general acceptance of the principle of "substitution by means of a representation." For this principle provided a solution for two basic problems: first, how to ensure that the dead king would have an eternal supply of food, utensils, and servants; and then, how to ensure that the king could safely receive the homage and tributes of his people.

Since the *ka* was a spiritual double, it was not bound by the physical limitations of a human being. It could pass through imitation doors made of stone or plaster; it could feed on things conveyed by image or word, not present in perishable, this-world actuality. This notion brought as much relief to the Egyptian economy as stimulus to the Egyptian artist. It was no longer necessary to load the king's tomb with real carcasses of oxen or ducks by the hundred thousand, nor to follow the barbarous practice of some other early societies and slay a horde of servants around his bier. It was enough to surround the dead with representations of food and servants; these would suffice to vitalize the *ka* and do its bidding.

As a result the artist became as important to Egyptian society as scientists are to ours. His hand and eye were responsible for the realistic bas-reliefs of animals, men, and objects that filled myriad tombs. Statuettes known as *ushabtis*, or answerers, were also provided to do any hard work that might crop up in the hereafter. These ghost-robots were called "answerers" because

The walls of the underground galleries of Zoser's Step Pyramid were lined with glazed ceramic tiles (far right) arranged to simulate rush matting. To enable Zoser's ka to receive offerings, while preserving his mortal remains below, a limestone portrait statue of the king (below) was placed in the offering chapel, or sirdab, adjoining his tomb. A common feature of later tombs was the inclusion of small mummy-like faience figurines known as ushabtis *(right), whose function was to serve the* ka *by performing in its stead whatever physical labors might be required of it.*

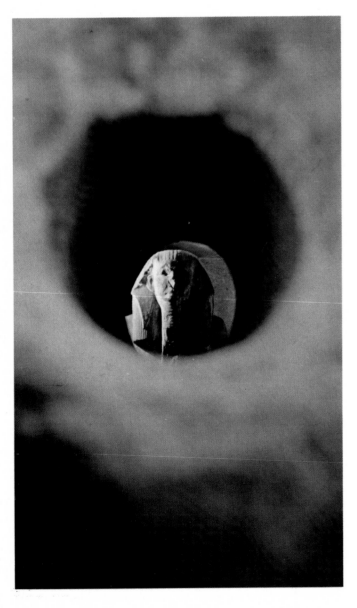

they were to answer in place of the dead Egyptian. A chapter of the *Book of the Dead* found in the tomb of a much later scribe expresses the principle: ". . . if I be called, or if I be adjudged to do any work whatsoever of the labors which are to be done in the underworld . . . let the judgment fall upon you instead of upon me always, in the matter of sowing the fields, of filling the canals with water, and of bringing fertilizer from the east to the west." To this the figure replies: "I am at your service wherever you command me."

But however well equipped the king might be in his deep-set tomb, it seemed to the Egyptian mind essential that he should receive, throughout eternity, visits from his people. This notion of visiting the dead was so deeply implanted that it would outlast the eclipse of the ancient world and flourish under a different theology into the present. For at major feasts of the year the people of Cairo still visit cemeteries — and the dead, although no longer embalmed (but laid, simply shrouded, in underground vaults), are still buried in houses that are replicas of earthly habitations.

Visiting a king had as its concomitant the offering of gifts and prayers — and this presented a serious problem. If the king's body and its costly accouterments were as accessible to the people as the relics of modern Catholic saints, they would be equally accessible to thieves. Yet if the body were buried safely far below ground, how could the *ka* know that he was being visited and in gratitude diffuse beneficence on his visitors? And what would the *ka* do if, by some horrendous chance, the corpse were destroyed or damaged?

The art of sculpture developed out of Egyptian answers to these practical considerations. Thanks to the

basic notion of the correspondence of likenesses, it was possible for a representation of the dead ruler, ritually endowed with his name, to stand as public proxy for his remote and secret corpse. His *ka* could glide up from the tomb and, passing through a false door, unbudging to human touch, could infuse the statue that permanently awaited homage in the tomb's offering chamber, or *sirdab*. The statue of Zoser discovered at Sakkara stands in such a *sirdab* to the north of the Step Pyramid. Opposite its rock-crystal eyes in their copper sockets are two openings in the chamber's wall; incense could reach the statue through the apertures, and the statue could gaze out of those openings at the fixed, circumpolar stars (known to ancient Egyptians as "those who know not death").

This use of statuary enabled kings to be deep-buried in response to the endless, and as we know vain, quest for mortuary safety. Statues were also a form of insurance against what in fact happened. The builders of the pyramids at Giza have survived as recognizable personalities thanks to the sculptor's art, although in the case of Cheops the representation that has survived is only a few inches tall. The bodies of all three kings have disappeared.

The development of the Egyptian royal tomb from a burial pit to the triumphant Great Pyramid is a logical sequence of responses to funerary needs. Take, for example, the reputed grave of Narmer's successor, King Aha, which has been excavated at Sakkara on the plateau overlooking Memphis. It is little more than a shallow pit, divided by five partitions. The king's body was once housed in its middle compartment, and the pit was roofed with wood. On top rose a brick super-structure divided into twenty-seven chambers for storing utensils and food. This oblong superstructure acquired the Arabic name *mastaba* in the nineteenth century when Egyptian villagers working for European archaeologists noticed a resemblance to the oblong mud-brick benches on which they sat gossiping in their village homes. The *mastaba* probably imitated the shape of ordinary dwellings of the archaic period.

In the next two dynasties the *mastaba* part of the tomb — the portion of the structure visible above-ground — had become a mere mass of rubble enclosed by stout retaining walls. At the same time the part of the tomb beneath the ground level had vastly expanded. The body itself was buried in a pit sunk deep into the rock. When the substitution of a statue had first been employed, the king's representation had stood at one end of the superstructure, on ground level. Bitter experience soon showed that statues were as liable to be robbed as corpses. As a protective measure the statue had to be placed in an underground chamber to which only priests had access.

Zoser's Step Pyramid at Sakkara marks one of those developments that afterward seem inevitable but that would have been impossible without an experimenting genius. That Imhotep was such a genius we know, not from Greek legend, which identified him with Aesculapius, the god of medicine, but from what archaeologists have discovered from his still impressive pyramid. Investigation has shown that, at every stage, he was prepared to experiment along new lines. His first innovation was to construct a *mastaba* that was not oblong, but square. His second concerned the material from which it was built. Hitherto brick had been

used for all buildings, though stone was used here and there for thresholds, floors, or lintels.

Imhotep decided to dress a core of Sakkara limestone with an outer casing of the superior stone from the quarries on the east bank of the Nile. The *mastaba* was 26 feet in height and its sides were 207 feet long, each side being oriented to one of the cardinal points. A dissatisfied Imhotep then extended his great square by about fourteen feet on all four sides. The extension was two feet lower than the original *mastaba,* so that a two-step structure now existed. This may have given Imhotep his next idea for an improvement. This was to enlarge the base and impose three diminishing squares on it to form a four-step pyramid. This still did not satisfy Imhotep or his royal patron, and the original four-step building was soon concealed inside a far more ambitious design — a great step pyramid of six platforms rising to a flat summit just over two hundred feet above ground level.

No document or inscription survives to explain why the true pyramid form was chosen for the monumental tombs of Egypt's kings, or why that form was finally achieved in the second pyramid built by Snofru, founder of the Fourth Dynasty, at Dahshur. (The first was rhomboid, or bent.) Several reasons have been inferred. Although apparently contradictory, these hypotheses are not mutually exclusive, since just as it was characteristic of Egyptians to allow Horus to coexist with Seth, so they probably allowed various insights to prompt their architectural designs.

Many architectural motifs in the buildings surrounding the Step Pyramid bear evidence of Mesopotamian influences. The great ziggurats dominating the Lower Euphrates skyline would have been remembered by those who traveled west to Egypt — much as they were remembered by the Hebrews in their legend of the Tower of Babel. Mesopotamia lacked stone; Egypt did not, and once the possibilities of building with stone were realized by the Egyptians, the construction of a man-made mountain in the relatively flat Egyptian landscape became an envisageable temptation. Nothing, they rightly saw, could be so impressive. A pyramid was also the logical development of Imhotep's design: a true pyramid being nothing more than a *mille feuille* step pyramid encased so as to present unbroken sides. To a people whose mathematics were already advanced, the appeal of a pure geometric figure must itself have been strong.

Two religious reasons may also have played their part. The king, as Horus, was associated with the cult of the sun-god, Re, whose shrine, "the fountain of the Sun," was at Heliopolis, now a suburb of Cairo and then a religious center known to the Egyptians and the Bible as On. The pyramid shape resembles the sun's rays as they often flare in Egypt, and an early religious text describes the king as using the sun's rays as ramps to ascend to heaven. There was a further link between the pyramid shape and the Re-worship at On in the *ben-ben,* an early sun symbol composed of a phoenix perching on a pyramidal plinth.

If the lack of written evidence forces us to guess why the pyramid shape was chosen, the written evidence as to how the pyramids were constructed is positively misleading. It was written by a man to whom the pyramids were older than the Colosseum is to us. Herodotus, the same Greek who identified Menes as the probable unifier of Egypt, was less fortunate in the information he gleaned at Giza. His informants were dragomans whom he mistook for priests, and as a result his trove combines uncheckable statistics to the effect that 100,000 men took thirty years to complete the Great Pyramid and its causeway. Picturesque details about the laborers' diet — radishes, onions, and garlic were dominant items — are included, as are details that we know to be untrue — such as that the builders used tools made of iron and that machines raised the stones from one level to another.

One story's inherent improbability is only rivaled by its charm:

The wickedness of Cheops reached to such a pitch that, when he had spent all his treasures and wanted more, he sent his daughter to the stews [brothels], with orders to procure him a certain sum — how much I cannot say, for I was not told; she procured it, however, and at the same time, bent on leaving a monument which should perpetuate her own memory, she required each man to make her a present of a stone towards the works which she contemplated. With these stones she built the pyramid which stands midmost of the three that are in front of the Great Pyramid, measuring along each side a hundred and fifty feet.

Fortunately the pyramids, including those of lesser importance farther south, embody clues as to how they were built. Patient excavation by modern archaeologists has made the pyramids' construction less mysterious than the origins of the kings who built them.

The pyramid builders had certain limited assets.

For one thing they could call on considerable reserves of labor. The figure mentioned by Herodotus — 100,000 men — is not impossible, and the Greek historian's remark that they were rotated in three-month shifts may be nothing more than a distorted recollection of the probable case that work on the pyramids proceeded in stages during the three summer months when the flooding Nile turned the valley into one huge lake. At that season agricultural work became impossible and the fellahin might well have been glad to work on any project that brought them rations of food, quite apart from the fact that such labor was a sacred task connected with the well-being of Egypt. The flooded Nile also made it possible to ferry to the western escarpment stone brought from the quarries of upriver Aswan as well as limestone from the quarries across the Nile Valley.

The greatest asset of the pyramid builders was an unsurpassed organizing talent. Two Western experts on ancient Egyptian building methods, architect Somers Clarke and engineer R. Engelbach, have flatly stated that the rulers of the Old Kingdom were "the best organizers of human labor the world has ever seen." This compliment does not seem excessive when the same experts further inform us that "the only mechanical appliances they knew were the lever, the roller, and the use of vast embankments." The split-second skill of the ancient overseers, a modern Egyptian authority on the pyramids has wryly remarked, seems the one talent that has disappeared.

The first task of the royal architects — which they probably shouldered early in each king's reign — was to select a site that met certain basic requirements. It

Proud monuments of a civilization that has long since disappeared, the three pyramids rise in breathtaking geometrical symmetry on the Giza plateau. Clustered in the foreground before Mycerinus's pyramid, the smallest of the three, are the satellite tombs of his immediate family. Chephren's pyramid (center), with its original limestone cap still in place, appears larger than the Great Pyramid to the rear because it sits on higher ground. In fact, Cheops's tomb is so vast that a party of schoolchildren (right) can scale its individual blocks only with considerable effort.

had to be on the western edge of the valley, since the evening ridge was the particular realm of the dead. It had to stand above the level of the highest floods, but not so high as to inhibit the ferrying of stone to within a convenient distance. It needed to be reasonably flat, and large enough to accommodate its suburb of courtiers' tombs. The rock must be solid and flawless in view of the giant burden it would have to bear. The local stone should be adequate for the hidden parts of the core.

The Giza plateau met these requirements perfectly.

The next stage was to peg out a base, which in the case of the Great Pyramid covered an area of just over thirteen acres. A knoll of projecting rock inside this area was incorporated into the bulk of added stone. The sides of the giant square, each roughly 755 feet long, faced the four cardinal points; the future entrance would look directly north to the Pole Star.

The next stage, the leveling of the base, was facilitated by techniques derived from Egyptian agriculture. Mud retaining walls such as those used in the valley fields were built around the pegged-out area and the space so formed filled with water. When the water covered all but the central knoll, a grid of trenches was excavated in the rock until the bottom of each trench was at the same distance from the surface of the water. This done, the mud walls were breached and the water allowed to escape. It was then possible to chip away the intervening rock between the trenches and so secure a level square with a protruding knoll around which the Great Pyramid would rise. This method of using water as a gigantic spirit level was so successful that the southeast corner of the pyramid stands only half an

inch higher than the northwest corner. Other dimensions were only slightly less precise, there being a difference of 7.9 inches between the longest side — the south — and the shortest side — the north.

If these dimensions reveal the calm confidence of men who had already achieved an effective calendar, the pyramid's internal design shows men still experimenting. Analysis of the pyramid has revealed their changes of plan. None of these changes affected the external appearance of the Great Pyramid (which retained the pure pyramidal form first achieved by Snofru, the father of Cheops, in his second pyramid at Dahshur) or altered the entrance site, which remained some fifty-five feet above ground level on the north.

The changes concerned the pyramid's main function: the storage of the royal cadaver. Imhotep had constructed Zoser's burial chamber deep in the solid rock beneath the Step Pyramid, and a similar mortuary plan was first devised for Cheops. An entrance corridor was designed to slant downward for almost 350 feet, first through the pyramid itself, then through the rock on which it stood. Finally a short horizontal passage led to a modest chamber, now choked with the rubble left by nineteenth-century explorers.

Only when the pyramid had advanced by several courses was a second plan made: to construct the chamber in the exact center of the pyramid, but not very high above ground level. It was now too late to plan for a corridor leading straight from the pyramid entrance to the pyramid's heart. Instead, the roof of the descending corridor was pierced and a new ascending corridor (the one in which you bend your back today) was constructed. This culminated, under the

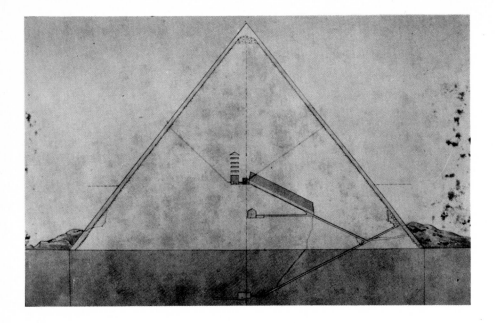

The nineteenth-century architectural cross-section at left reveals the three-stage evolution of the interior design of the Great Pyramid, culminating in the construction of the King's Chamber at its center. At right is an idealized drawing of the structures that formed a typical pyramid complex.

second plan, in a horizontal passage leading to the misnamed Queen's Chamber, intended for Cheops. (His queens were in fact buried under the three smaller pyramids that still survive to the east of the Great Pyramid.) This second attempt was next abandoned for a third, more ambitious design — one that involved the construction of the Grand Gallery with its corbeled roof and King's Chamber of granite.

No improvisation such as had modified the corridor system for the second plan was involved in the third. The Gallery and King's Chamber were built from plans as the pyramid nudged skyward, layer by layer. Wooden scaffolding, erected inside the Grand Gallery, supported great stone plugs that could be lowered immediately after the funeral so as to block forever the ascending corridor. The workmen responsible for closing off the Gallery arranged for their own future: a well-like shaft was bored down to meet the original descending corridor in the rock; having sealed the access route they could then escape, pulling a trapdoor after them.

It was long a puzzle how more than two million stones — the nine granite slabs roofing the King's Chamber average forty-four tons — were raised on the ascending layers. Most historians reached the conclusion that a Greek contemporary of Julius Caesar, Diodorus Siculus, was on the right track when he wrote that the pyramid had been constructed by the use of "mounds," or ramps. His view was theoretically endorsed by Somers Clarke and Engelbach, since they knew that the Old Kingdom Egyptians, who lacked practical knowledge of the wheel, capstan, and pulley, had relied on manpower for most of their haulage.

This view found practical confirmation when the unfinished step pyramid of a successor to Zoser was excavated at Sakkara. Ramps made of rubble and builders' waste were found still in place. The remains of one such ramp almost certainly underlie the road by which the modern visitor approaches the Giza plateau.

These ramps were probably of two kinds. Long, broad supply mounds gave an easy incline for the blocks of cut stone, which were edged forward on rollers whose only lubricants were milk or water. Shorter, more sharply pitched ramps probably raised workmen and lighter materials close to the working face. The outer casing, which filled the triangular gap between each layer and the next, was probably laid stage by stage as the work rose higher. When the apex had been reached and the granite capstone placed in position, the ramp would have been removed and the limestone casing smoothed and polished till a seamless sheet reflected the sun by day and the moon by night.

The completed pyramids of Cheops, Chephren, and Mycerinus were not in ancient times the isolated monoliths they now seem. Each vast tomb was the key component, the radioactive pile, in a complex of buildings that may be understood as a spiritual reactor. The whole could not function properly without a number of important constituents.

A convenient way to describe the complex is to start where the body of the dead king may have started its funeral journey, at the intersection of the desert and the sown fields. A valley temple stood at the edge of the living vegetation that the god-king was first to leave and later to bless. This valley temple was reached by a canal, and when the king died he was probably brought

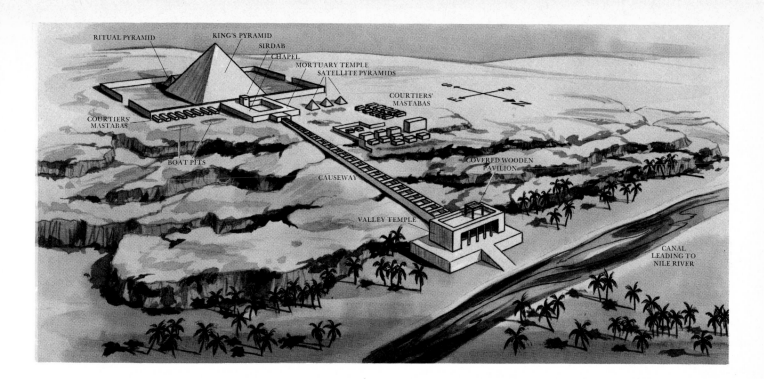

RITUAL PYRAMID | KING'S PYRAMID
SIRDAB
CHAPEL
MORTUARY TEMPLE
SATELLITE PYRAMIDS
COURTIERS'
MASTABAS
COURTIERS'
MASTABAS
BOAT PITS
COVERED WOODEN
PAVILION
CAUSEWAY
VALLEY TEMPLE
CANAL
LEADING TO
NILE RIVER

to the temple by barge for three important ceremonies. The first was concerned with ritual purity, always important in Egyptian religion (as the derivation of the word for priest from a root meaning "pure" implies). Just as the sun was believed to wash in a lake of lilies before being reborn each morning, the dead king required ritual cleansing on the boundary between death and rebirth.

The next, longer-lasting task was to prepare his body for its eternity of repose. During the Old Kingdom elaborate techniques of mummification were still unknown. The internal organs, being the most perishable, were removed and stored separately in what are known as canopic jars. Such perishable features as the face, the breasts, and the genital organs were modeled in cloth before the body was swathed in tight linen bandages. It is uncertain where the process of embalming was carried out, but it may have been in a wooden pavilion on the valley temple roof. Its completion took a considerable time — on rare occasions it lasted the full nine months of the human gestation period. Then the body was ready for the last and most important ceremony, The Opening of the Mouth. The king's purified, embalmed body was borne into a T-shaped central hall and laid in front of statues of himself. Magic was now employed to associate him with each of these statues. Priests, whose number included at least one of the deceased ruler's sons, conducted rituals believed to endow the statues with a simulacrum of life. Each statue in turn was sprinkled, censed, and offered sacrifice; its mouth was next touched with adze and chisel, then rubbed with milk. Decked with the emblems of royalty, each statue could

then receive the dead king's *ka* and stand proxy for his body throughout all ages.

An expanse of sand and rock lay between the valley temple and the pyramid high on the western escarpment. Since the king was now ritually pure, and indeed an embodiment of Osiris, profane eyes must not see his funeral cortege. An enclosed stone causeway enabled the king's wooden coffin to be carried unseen on its final journey from the valley. The causeway of the Great Pyramid no longer remains, but we know that it was lined with painted reliefs and roofed against the sun, light entering through horizontal slits. Its building reputedly took ten years, or half as long as the pyramid it served.

The causeway led to the mortuary temple. Each mortuary temple that has been excavated differs slightly from all others, but its functions were the same. An innermost shrine focused on a statue backing a false door through which the *ka* could emerge from the tomb inside the pyramid. The mortuary temple was normally built close to the pyramid's eastern face; in Chephren's case, however, there was an intervening area of paving. The mortuary temple was the focus of the cult of the dead king once he was entombed inside his pyramid. Here the priests would daily deposit a meal in the innermost shrine; only the essence of the food would be tasted by the *ka*; the untouched remains would be removed the following morning and replaced. The mortuary temple had a main courtyard. Here worshipers could address much the same prayers — for recovery from sickness, for success in business, for fruitfulness in marriage — as are offered in other countries to other gods or saints.

The pyramid was protected from the sand by a paved court enclosed by a wall. On the north side, near the entrance through which the king's body had disappeared, stood a small chapel; on the south was a small ritual pyramid, unconnected with burial. Around the main pyramid boat-shaped pits concealed the ships that the king would need in the hereafter.

Each of the pyramids at Giza shows some aspects of the complex. A newly discovered boat pit has revealed an intact, although dismantled, boat belonging to Cheops. The valley temple of Chephren is impressively substantial, with polished red granite facing local limestone; Chephren's mortuary temple, though much ruined, has left a discernible plan; and the battered substance of Chephren's causeway is still extant. But those wishing to see a pyramid complex more or less complete must journey a dozen miles south to Sakkara. Immediately to the southwest of Zoser's enclosure rises the modest, ruined pyramid of Unas. His causeway, partially intact, partially restored, gives an awesome impression as it sweeps from his valley temple in a curving line 730 yards long to the mortuary temple. The causeway takes depressions and gullies in its stride, being embanked over previous tombs on a lower level. On the walls of the easily entered burial chamber is inscribed the earliest of the pyramid texts.

King Unas reigned some two centuries after Cheops. By then the Old Kingdom was already falling apart and some of its monuments were in disrepair. In fact, some of the stones that Unas used to embank his causeway were lifted from Zoser's enclosure. Unas stands at the junction point of the Fifth Dynasty with the Sixth. After the Sixth Dynasty Egyptian history fades into a period of still shadowy inexactitude that Egyptologists term the First Intermediate Period. The monuments that the Old Kingdom monarchs had built to ensure and exploit their immortality probably contributed to the collapse of Egypt's centralized power.

A pyramid was not only expensive to build; as a functioning complex — staffed by priests, supplied with food, and protected by guards — it needed large funds for maintenance. The kings secured such funds by setting aside large estates whose revenues would support these ancient equivalents of medieval abbeys or cathedrals. This diverted a vast amount of land into the hands of individuals remote from Memphis. And in a land where reverence and self-interest have often coexisted, this meant that regional officials had at their disposal increasing wealth, and therefore power. This completely altered the psychological atmosphere of the Egypt that Narmer had united. In the heyday of Snofru and Cheops officials had no higher ambition than to have a tomb near the royal enclosure; they were content for their humble *mastabas* to be as dwarfed by the pyramid as the stars seem dwarfed by the sun. But as they grew rich, with whole provinces at their command, they were no longer content with humility in this world and the next. These new feudal lords began to plan for their personal immortality; private tombs were erected all over Egypt. From its traces in architecture and written documents, this Intermediate Period seems to some historians the one period of individualism in the history of ancient Egypt. But it certainly marked the extinction of the qualities that had made the Old Kingdom and its permanent symbols, the pyramids of Giza, unique.

*King Ay assumes priestly garb (above) to perform
the final funerary rite — The Opening of the Mouth —
for his predecessor, Tutankhamen. The dead king,
reborn as Osiris, could then join such immortals as
Shu, god of the air. In the papyrus opposite,
Shu creates the world by separating the star-speckled
body of the sky-goddess from the prostrate earth-god.*

III

Horus-in-the-Horizon

The Egyptian genius for visual metaphor — the ability to hold two separate images in the mind and then connect them — achieved its boldest triumph in the Sphinx. This colossal image dates from the lifetime of Chephren, builder of the second Giza pyramid.

The Sphinx was probably conceived in three distinct stages. First, some unrecorded foreman or even workman noticed that a projection of limestone in the quarried area to the south of the pyramid of Cheops resembled a lion. Standing immediately to the north of Chephren's causeway and within a hundred yards of the site of his valley temple, the rocky knoll was an obstruction. It would have to be leveled and its stone used for the hidden portions of Chephren's pyramid — unless it could be put to some other use. The chief architect was probably asked the question: have not the late king's quarriers left what already resembles the king of beasts?

To urban, twentieth-century man, the lion is an exotic rarity associated with zoos or millionaires' safaris, a threatened creature for whose preservation we feel concern. To the ancient Egyptians, however, the lion was a dangerous being who could more than look after himself. He was, if no longer a rival of men, then a rival of yesterday. Sporting statistics from reigns fifteen centuries after Chephren's show that lions were still the plentiful prey of royal hunts.

This first intuition — that the rock resembled a lion — was no different from the associations made by modern picnickers with clouds or tree shapes. The second and peculiarly Egyptian intuition was to relate the leonine shape to the king whose pyramid complex was then being built. This association had roots far older than Chephren's time; predynastic slate palettes show that the ruler could be represented as a lion no less than as a hawk. One such palette shows a lion undermining the foundations of a fortified town with a digging tool.

The lion not only symbolized ferocious strength — although this association was never to pale — he was also the supreme guardian. Representations of a lion were substituted for the prosaic timbers of household furniture. His paws formed the feet of chairs; his body, stretched out to form a bed, provided the securest slumber; and since death was the mirror image of life, he similarly provided the ideal bier.

A tamed lion accompanied the king into battle; much more than a mascot, he represented the reassuring presence of a god. For the lion had earlier been incorporated into divinity. Ptah, the god of Memphis, belonged to a triad whose other members, Nefer-Atum and Sekhmet, both had leonine associations. Nefer-Atum was portrayed standing on a lion, while his mother, Sekhmet, had a lioness's head. Curiously, the lion was also linked with moisture (through Tefnut, lion-headed goddess of rain and dew). This association probably derived from the zodiacal sign of Leo, since it was during his summer month that the Nile began to flood. In Europe that conception is reflected in the persistent use of a lion's head as a waterspout.

After these two intuitions came a third stage, the stage of accomplishment. A large body of skilled workers was employed to fashion the rock into an image of the king of Upper and Lower Egypt — represented as part man, part lion. The body, with outstretched paws and stocky encircling tail, was 66 feet high and 240

Only the head and shoulders of the Great Sphinx were visible above the encroaching desert sands in the nineteenth century.
Overleaf:
Fully exposed in the twentieth century, the enormous crouching figure looms majestically between the pyramids of Chephren (left) and Cheops (right).

feet long. The vast head — the nose roughly the height of an average Egyptian, the enigmatic lips more than seven feet across — embodied the idealized features of Chephren. The presence of a pleated headdress, a uraeus or rampant cobra, and an Osiris beard completed a "living image" that fused king, lion, and man.

The sounds for the Egyptian phrase "living image" have been transliterated by Alan Gardiner as *šspᶜnh* — or more pronounceably by Selim Hassan as *sheshep-ankh;* they almost certainly give us our word sphinx. The hieroglyphs with which they were written contain pictograms indicating godhead and eternal life. By the time the first inscriptions mentioning the Sphinx occur, long after it was constructed, the link with a particular king was forgotten and the huge statue was known as Hor-am-Akhet, Horus-in-the-Horizon; from this the Greeks derived Harmachis, the name they gave to the god of the Sphinx.

The link with the horizon takes us straight back to the world of Egyptian metaphor, for ancient Egyptian, written as it was in hieroglyphs, embodied history's first "concrete poetry." The association with the horizon was double. The western horizon, the edge of the desolate Sahara, was the province of Osiris, and its Egyptian name, Kheret-neter-Akhet-Khufu, or Necropolis of the Horizon of Khufu (Cheops), was commonly used as a euphemism for the Giza burial area. The second link was visual. The hieroglyph for horizon shows a sun disk between two hills. This approximates the large circle of the Sphinx's head lying as it does between two hills.

Scholars have long debated whether the Sphinx was from the start a god in its own right. Such argument,

logical in the context of Western ideas, would have meant little to the Egyptians with their fluidity of thought. But the ruins of the Sphinx Temple, built during the Fourth Dynasty, prove that divine honors were paid to the image from the time of its construction. Fashioned from cyclopean blocks, many of which are three times larger than the average building blocks of the Great Pyramid, the Sphinx Temple is the oldest nonmortuary temple so far discovered in Egypt. In keeping with a period when the unification of Egypt was still comparatively recent, its features emphasize duality. There are, for example, two entrances, two outer passages, two sets of chambers in the western wall. In much the same way, the ruler of unified Egypt took as one of his titles the odd phrase "Two Ladies," referring to the vulture and the cobra, patronesses of Upper and Lower Egypt respectively.

The excavation of this ruined temple has solved one enduring puzzle about the Sphinx. Votive stelae discovered in the nearby sands, gifts of pilgrims whose prayers the Sphinx had granted, show the creature reposing on a pedestal. That pedestal is, in fact, an early exploitation of optical illusion. The Sphinx is part and parcel of the rock from which it was carved; there is no pedestal, nor have persistent digging and scarring revealed intestinal hollows or subterranean crypts stacked with treasure.

The illusion of a pedestal was achieved as follows: the rock from which the Sphinx was carved and on which it seems to lie was cut down in front to some eight feet below paw level. This drop of smoothed rock was then incorporated into the western wall of the Sphinx Temple, so that a pilgrim entering the

temple courtyard from the east beheld a spectacular vision of the Sphinx reposing on what seemed to be a large pedestal. A concave cornice just below the paws abetted the illusion.

During the centuries in which the Sphinx was more or less covered with drifted sand, people speculated about the construction of the statue and what underlay it. Some suggested that the Sphinx, like other gigantic statues, had been constructed elsewhere and conveyed hither. An inscription dating from the second century A.D. indicates that by the twilight of Egyptian civilization the Sphinx was popularly regarded as a construction of the gods:

> Your fearful form is the work of the deathless gods.
> To spare the flat and fertile lands
> They placed you in your depression,
> A rocky island from which they banished the sand.
> They placed you as a neighbor to the pyramids,
> Not like the sphinx of Thebes, killed by Oedipus,
> But as a holy servant of Horus-Apollo
> Who vigilantly watches the blessed Osiris. . . .

So unforgettable an image sent ripples of influence, imitation, and misunderstanding through later millennia. A vast progeny of composite creatures inside and outside Egypt have their ancestry in the enigmatic guardian of the Giza necropolis.

Not all subsequent Egyptian sphinxes were male. A female sphinx — beardless, her face painted the indoor yellow shared by women with the god Ptah — has been discovered at Abu Roash, site of the most northerly pyramid, a tomb associated with Chephren's elder half brother. It may represent a Fourth Dynasty queen

and could even be older than the Giza male. Nor were all Egyptian sphinxes couchant and benign. The daughter of Mycerinus (who built the third Giza pyramid) erected a fourth major structure at Giza in whose ruins were found the vestiges of a rampant sphinx.

Later sphinxes are often difficult to date since a new ruler frequently purloined the statues of his predecessors. Some of the most interesting of these are the so-called Tanis sphinxes, in which only the mask is human, while the furry ears and mane of a lion replace human ears and royal headdress. (The powerful features of the Tanis sphinxes are probably those of Amenhemet III, a great Twelfth Dynasty king.) Still later dynasties reemphasized the aggressive aspect of the lion — so that a gentle and delicate boy-king who never went within a hundred miles of a battle was depicted as a voracious sphinx, prancing over his Nubian enemies. Nor was the sphinx always human-faced. A special variety, the criosphinx, incorporated the head of a ram, the emblem of the god Amen-Re who was to dominate the last two thousand years of ancient Egyptian history. An avenue of such sphinxes survives outside the great temple at Karnak, near the modern city of Luxor.

Foreign sculptors often seized upon the less typical aspects of this fascinating creature — and while western Asian sphinxes were grotesque fusions of beasts and birds, it was the Greeks who made the most radical and consistent departure from the Giza ideal. Most Egyptian sphinxes had been male, wingless, and benign, but Greek sphinxes were female, winged, and malign. The Greeks, unaware of the derivation of the word sphinx from "living image," instead derived

it — perhaps through some function of the collective unconscious — from their own verb *sphingein,* meaning to strangle or squeeze. The sphinx in the Oedipus legend was such a monster. She perched on the cliffs overlooking the Greek town of Thebes and strangled all males who failed to answer her riddle. This riddle, and her reputed origin in Africa, clearly link her with Egypt. "What," she asked Oedipus, "is the creature that walks on four legs in the morning, two legs at noon and three in the evening?" The answer — man — was a remembrance of the Egyptian distinction between the three phases of the sun, each with its own title: Kheperi, the infant sun of morning; Re, the powerful sun of noon; and Atum, the enfeebled but creative sun of evening.

An equally radical misunderstanding of the Sphinx was shown by the Arabs, shapers of modern Egypt. Because of their taboo on representative art, the Arabs did not copy the Sphinx; instead, they bequeathed it a name that marks the final alienation of the Egyptians from their ancient gods. Asking seventh-century Egyptians "What on earth is this?" the Arabs had been told: Per-Hol, Place of Hol. Hol, or Hor, meant not only Horus, but Horan, a Syrian deity whose devotees had built a settlement near the Sphinx. (That community survives as the modern Egyptian village of Horania.) The Arabs identified Hol, not with the hawk-god of order and justice, but with their own word for terror. Consequently, the Sphinx is known to modern Egyptians as Abul-Hol, or The Father of Terror.

To the men who built it the Sphinx of Giza was a symbol of good. Around it centered one of the many persistent Egyptian attempts to reach an understanding of the unity behind phenomena. A stele erected by a director of works during the Twenty-second Dynasty (945–730 B.C.) is inscribed:

> Hail to you, King of the Gods, Atum Kheperi, in the beginning, self-begetting as sole lord, the primal unity with no companion: making the names of the gods before mountains and desert, making the things under earth, all in a flash, planning, forming, no other god with you. You made the secret underworld. . . . You lead the earth. You lifted the sky to raise your soul under your name of High One. You built a fortress of hidden name in the holy desert. Daily, forever, you rise as morning before them.

As it rises beyond the valley of the living every morning, the sun strikes the forehead of the Sphinx. The face thus lit up — some rough red ochre yet coloring its battered cheeks — embodies mystery, humor, and awe, not terror or doom.

IV
Imperial High Noon

Egypt, however blessed by Nile and sun, is a country where without watchful care things fall to pieces. The blessedness is itself a drug. Three intermediate periods of chaos or misrule punctuate the march of the dynasties from the unification of Egypt to the death of Cleopatra (see chronology, pages 162–63). In each the records and dates become vague. The first such intermediate period marked the end of the Old Kingdom and the second marked the end of the Middle Kingdom, which had been dominated by the creative Twelfth Dynasty. The third followed the collapse of the Egyptian empire and the end of the Ramesside dynasties. Such times of dereliction had a natural ally in the *khamsin,* the harsh spring wind that blows tons of Libyan sand across the valley and delta and makes May the least agreeable month in the Egyptian year.

The Sphinx has always been a particular victim of these eddying sands. Photographs taken in the nineteenth century show the mammoth statue buried almost up to the neck, its paws covered. That the Sphinx had been in a similarly scruffy condition thirty-four centuries earlier we know from a granite tablet placed against its leonine chest by the fifteenth-century-B.C. ruler who first cleared the sand away.

That granite tablet, or stele, tells how a young prince, a member of a dynasty ruling Egypt from the relatively new southern capital of Thebes, took particular pleasure in visiting the desert overlooking the old capital of Memphis. He came there to shoot at a target with copper bolts as well as to hunt lions and the smaller desert game. The prince drove to the escarpment in a prized innovation, a horse-drawn chariot that he drove faster than the winds. Unlike previous princes, he was simply attended, bringing with him only two companions. One thing had not changed: the Egyptian climate imposed a siesta.

So far we have paraphrased the stele. Now we may quote directly:

> On one such day it so happened that the king's son Tuthmosis had come hunting at noon and afterwards rested in the shadow of this great god. Sleep seized him and he found the majestic deity speaking to him as a father speaks to his child. "Look at me, Tuthmosis my son: I am your father, Horus-in-the-Horizon, Kheperi-Re-Atum. I promise what is in my gift: earthly rule at the head of all the living. Seated on the throne of the earth-god you will wear the White Crown and the Red. All the territory on which the eye of the sun rests will be yours: yours the food of the Two Lands, great tribute and long life. To you I turn my face and heart for protection, since I am sick in all my limbs. The sands of the holy place upon which I rest have covered me. . . ."

In the first year of his reign as Tuthmosis IV the young man had the sand cleared from the Sphinx's limbs; mud-brick retaining walls were designed to prevent the sand from seeping back. The Sphinx kept its side of the bargain less generously: Tuthmosis had a reign of no more than eight years. Compared with other members of his dynasty he achieved little. He did erect the tallest obelisk in the world in the temple of Amen-Re, the Theban god. But that obelisk, which now stands outside St. John Lateran in Rome, had been fashioned by his grandfather, Tuthmosis III, who also commissioned the three shafts that now stand in

This granite stele commemorates Tuthmosis IV's prophetic dream in the shadow of the Sphinx.

the Istanbul Hippodrome, by the Thames in London, and in New York's Central Park.

Nevertheless, the young ruler's interests were typical of members of his family, most of whom were wiry athletes and indefatigable hunters. Like them, he took part in routine foreign campaigns, donating a colony of Asiatics captured in Palestine to the upkeep of his mortuary temple. In one area, religion, he stands out as an individual. Perhaps permanently influenced by his dream near the Sphinx, he showed particular attachment to the sun cult of the north. On a giant commemorative scarab he spoke of the sun's disk, or Aten, stating that he led his army with the Aten before him.

The most striking thing about Tuthmosis IV is his position both in time and at the center of a tangle of family relationships. His reign (circa 1425–1417 B.C.) falls approximately halfway between the first Egyptian dynasty and the last. To him the Sphinx was as ancient as relics of Charlemagne or Justinian are to us. He was probably unaware that the Sphinx's features had been carved to represent Chephren, builder of the second pyramid. His account of the Sphinx's words shows that he identified Horus-in-the-Horizon with the sun in its three phases. "It is extremely doubtful," Selim Hassan, an Egyptian authority on the Sphinx, has written, "if there was a single person living in Egypt at this period who knew as much of the true history of the Sphinx as we do today."

Tuthmosis IV also falls halfway through the list of rulers of the Eighteenth Dynasty, the most remarkable family to rule since the Old Kingdom (see genealogical chart, page 54). It is questionable if any ruler in history, not excluding the first Roman Caesars, had such varied and talented relations. His great-grandmother was Hashepsowe (also known as Hatshepsut), a strong-willed, art-loving woman who reigned not as queen but as king. In her official portraits Hashepsowe is shown flat-breasted and wearing masculine regalia — including the ritual beard of plaited hair "held at the point of the chin by a strap on each side, which passed round the jaw and in front of the ear and was attached to the crown itself." The boy-king's grandfather, Tuthmosis III — nephew, coregent, and supplanter of this redoubtable woman — was Egypt's greatest military genius, a Napoleon-sized conqueror who left the first coherent account of a decisive battle.

Tuthmosis IV's immediate descendants, products of his marriage to the daughter of the King of Mitanni, a powerful new state in northern Syria, were no less arresting. His son by his foreign queen was Amenhotep III, builder of colossal statues in which he and his nonroyal wife, Tiye, are posed as equals (unlike most earlier groups, in which a queen might be a quarter the size of her spouse). One unforgettable late portrait — a bitter comedown from such colossi as still stand on the west bank of the Nile, facing Luxor — shows Amenhotep III looking like a weary and corpulent chairman of some giant corporation.

The son of Amenhotep III and Tiye was the greatest eccentric in Egyptian history, the heretic who, by changing his name from Amenhotep to Akhenaten, incorporated into his new title the Aten that his grandfather had honored. Some further family relationships have still not been resolved to scholars' universal agreement, thanks to the custom of using the term "father" in a complimentary as well as a genealogical

The boy-king Tuthmosis IV (left) was one of the few pharaohs immortalized in stone beside his mother rather than his wife. Tuthmosis' luxury-loving son Amenhotep III constructed a mile-long artificial lake near his palace at Thebes in honor of his chief consort, the formidable Queen Tiye. The statue of the royal pair at right is about thirty-six feet high; the child at their feet is actually twice life-size.

sense. It is nevertheless probable that another grandson of Tuthmosis IV was the boy-king Tutankhamen, whose funerary treasure has illuminated the tastes of a dynasty rivaled for opulence only by the Bourbons.

This outstanding family, with its characteristically oval-shaped faces, large noses, and insubstantial builds, presided over a renaissance of Egyptian power, a transformation of Egyptian culture, and, ironically, the first intimations of final decline.

The family originated in Upper Egypt, the base for a long and ultimately successful struggle to purge and reunite the country, after a period of misrule which was in some ways graver than the chaos that had followed the disintegration of the Old Kingdom. For nearly two centuries at least part of Egypt had been ruled by foreign kings known as the Hyksos. The Egyptian words *heka khasewt* mean "chieftains of a foreign hill country," and the hilly terrain from which the Hyksos derived was almost certainly Palestine and Syria. Although alien to Egypt, the Hyksos succumbed to its persuasive culture and reigned in their turn as god-kings. Significantly, they chose as their patron Seth, the desert deity who was the opponent of Horus, and they built their capital in the delta — close to Sinai and the road to the east.

Scholars have conjectured that the biblical story of Joseph, also a Palestinian entering Egypt in times of hardship, may derive from this period. The rise of the ruler "who knew not Joseph" may relate to the Egyptian national counterattack, for resistance to the Hyksos had crystalized in the south, then as now the nursery of the hardiest Egyptians. In the sixteenth century before Christ the first Eighteenth Dynasty ruler, Ahmose,

managed to expel the Hyksos from Egypt while his subjects, with a mechanism typical of their culture, expelled them from memory. What little we know of the deleted Hyksos period we know from archaeological fragments and scholarly conjecture.

The same mechanism of deletion, an ancient foreshadowing of George Orwell's "memory chute," in due time erased the Eighteenth Dynasty's two most interesting members: the masculine queen Hashepsowe and the feminine king Akhenaten.

Hashepsowe was married to Tuthmosis II, an unimpressive ruler. A court official has left us a terse account of his death:

> Having ascended into heaven, he became united with the gods and his son, having arisen in his place as king of the Two Lands, ruled upon the throne of his begetter, while his sister, the god's wife Hashepsowe, governed the country and the Two Lands were under her control; people worked for her, and Egypt bowed the head.

Although ancient Egypt was less male-assertive than some later societies (and inheritance through the mother was a normal pattern), we can sense a note of resentment at a female ruler. Part of this resentment may have been due to primordial associations of the king's reproductive organs with the fertility of herds and crops. Hashepsowe was aware of such feelings, hence her desire to be portrayed as a male — as a kneeling granite statue or a male sphinx. Yet something feminine affects the beast's expression.

This great woman was more interested in architecture and commerce than foreign conquest. At Deir

THE EIGHTEENTH DYNASTY

Royal incest was openly and systematically practiced throughout the three-thousand-year history of pharaonic Egypt, but it reached its apogee during the illustrious Eighteenth Dynasty. As this simplified genealogical chart indicates, there were at least six instances of regal inbreeding in the space of ten generations. Three occurred in succession during the first half of the dynasty, as Tuthmosis I, his namesake, and his grandson married their half sisters Ahmes, Hashepsowe, and Neferura, respectively. The heretic-king Akhenaten, whose distinctive physique reflects those incestuous unions, was content to wed his first cousin Nefertiti. But when their marriage produced no male heir, the slack-bellied pharaoh attempted to ensure the succession by marrying two of his daughters to his half brothers Smenkhare and Tutankhamen.

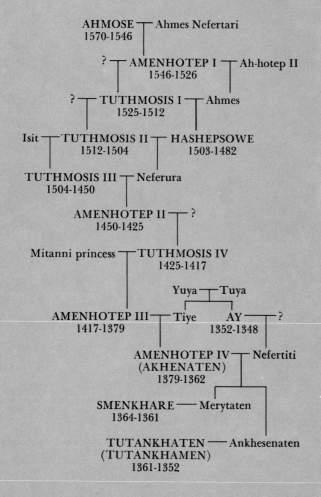

When the boy-king Tutankhamen died unexpectedly in 1352 B.C., leaving no male heir to the throne, power passed to Queen Ankhesenaten's maternal grandfather, the shrewd and ambitious King Ay. He was succeeded by a minor noble named Horemheb (1348-1320), last pharaoh of the dynasty.

el-Bahri she created a mortuary temple that compares with the pyramids for spectacular scope and rivals them for its imaginative use of landscape. The motive prompting her to build was the same one that had prompted Zoser, Snofru, and Cheops: after twelve centuries the same metaphysical imperatives governed the disposal of a dead Egyptian ruler, whether male or female. The body must be kept safe for the regeneration of the *ka;* there must be a place, not too far removed from the embalmed corpse, where the *ka* could receive its tributes of sacrifice and prayer.

By the Twelfth Dynasty, the building of royal pyramids had ceased in Egypt. (Much later, at Merowe in the Sudan, an Ethiopian dynasty would resume building them.) In its role as bank vault the pyramid had proved a costly failure. The pyramid clusters along the west bank of the Nile had acted as giant signposts to hidden treasure — signposts that had been followed by the impious in times of order and by the opportunistic in times of chaos. With the removal of Egypt's capital to the south in the wake of the wholesale destruction of temples by the Hyksos, the Eighteenth Dynasty made new responses to the old metaphysical demands. These new responses were suggested by the rugged landscape across the river from the temples and palaces of Thebes. Beyond a narrow but verdant plain rose the harshly beautiful battlements of the west, very different from the featureless plateau of Giza. Behind a 1,300-foot-high peak curled a bleak, easily guarded valley destined to become the richest repository of treasure in human history.

Instead of advertising their "houses of eternity," the Theban rulers concealed them at the ends of long

Hashepsowe's chief minister, Senmut, is portrayed in this block statue with his royal pupil, the queen's daughter, on his knees. The two heads emerging from the confines of the massive granite block convey an aura of tender affection between tutor and pupil.
  Overleaf:
In designing Hashepsowe's lavish terraced mortuary temple in the Valley of the Kings, Senmut took full advantage of the natural drama of the site.

underground burrows. Brilliantly decorated inside — probably with the help of mirrors that threw sunlight deep underground — these shaft-tombs had no entrance temples. Instead, once stoppered after the funeral, the entrances were made to resemble the rocky surface of the barren valley. On the eastern side of the high cliff, in full view of the fertile valley, were the visitable temples of the buried rulers. Here, too, in a honeycomb of tombs, were buried their nobles.

Hashepsowe had first conceived the bold idea of driving her burrow eastward, straight under the mountain; in this way her sarcophagus and that of her divine father, Tuthmosis, could lie under the cliff itself. She planned to transform the sheer face of the escarpment into a vast temple, imitating on a far grander scale the mortuary temple built by an Eleventh Dynasty predecessor. But the tunnel collapsed and this part of her scheme had to be abandoned. Hashepsowe's ultimate design — an ascending sequence of colonnaded courtyards culminating in a rock-hewn inner shrine — served the same functions as the mortuary temples attached to the pyramids. But whereas the pyramids were large objects posed on the Giza plateau, her temple exploited an unrivaled natural site to make a complex of momentous impact.

Reliefs in the temple show both Hashepsowe's need to bolster her regnal rights and her commercial interests. For example, one series shows her divine conception. (In the fluid context of Egyptian beliefs there need be no contradiction in the queen's claim to be at once the physical daughter of Tuthmosis I and the metaphysical daughter of the god Amen-Re.) Other reliefs show a trading expedition to the "Land of Punt," a country situated somewhere near the horn of Africa. Egyptian ships had probably been carried in pieces over the desert and assembled on the shore of the Red Sea. After navigating the Red Sea and the straits near modern Aden, the sailors made landfall near a community of Africans shown as living in round domed huts standing on stilts. The African ruler had a wife as monstrously overweight as the ladies reported to loll in the king of Uganda's harem in the nineteenth century. The Africans abased themselves before the standards of the Egyptian queen. "They speak, praying for peace from her Majesty: Hail to thee, king of Egypt, female sun who shinest like the solar disk. . . ."

Egyptian inscriptions rarely recorded unharmonious facts; they give no indication of how the queen's reign may have been terminated by supporters of Tuthmosis III, Hashepsowe's nephew and coregent, now grown to manhood. Whether Hashepsowe died of natural causes, was retired, or was murdered is still unknown. But some time after the king assumed solitary power he had every artistic reference to Hashepsowe that he could uncover destroyed.

Hashepsowe's interests in art and commerce, set against her nephew's interests in war and the establishment of Egyptian hegemony in western Asia, exemplify — on one level — the external differences between male and female. (The Greeks symbolized those differences in their fable of how Achilles, dressed for his safety as a girl, involuntarily snatched at the weapons proffered by the artful Odysseus, thus betraying his disguise.) The differences can also be understood on another level. Hashepsowe was reverting to the behavior of the pyramid builders, to an age when

Egypt could more safely disregard the outside world except as a source for stone, copper, ostrich feathers, and slaves. The Twelfth Dynasty — in its role as reviver of national unity after a period of breakdown — had also attempted to confine its main interest to Egypt. Such attitudes had been appropriate to the third millennium B.C. At that time Egypt was virtually isolated in a world where the only comparable cultures were situated in the distant valleys of the Euphrates and Indus. Her immediate neighbors — nomadic Libyans to the west, Nubian kinglets to the south, and starveling Bedouins to the east — were ineffective enough to be despised — and dismissed without fear.

In its daily life, religion, and art the Egypt that Tuthmosis III inherited superficially resembled the earlier kingdoms, but the world in which it stood had radically changed. The Egypt that had only recently expelled the Hyksos now shared the Middle East with innumerable small states in Syria and Palestine — and beyond these, the growing powers of the Mitanni on the Upper Euphrates and the Hittites in mountainous Anatolia. These new, developed societies, using techniques and materials more advanced than those found in Egypt, confronted a conservative culture with the threat of a new domination equivalent to that of the hated Hyksos.

The response of Tuthmosis III was a forward policy that made him one of the great military leaders of history. The system he consolidated — which lasted through the Eighteenth and Nineteenth dynasties — is often referred to as the New Empire. This term fits if it is taken to imply external involvement and an enforced hegemony. An empire in the Roman sense could have been established only if large numbers of Egyptians had been prepared to settle in Palestine and Syria. This did not happen. Throughout their history Egyptians have shown reluctance to populate even the oases near their immediate area; their valley and delta have seemed too delightful to leave. Making no effort to create such a Roman-style empire, Tuthmosis established a *pax Aegyptica* from northern Syria to northern Sudan. This was based on commissioners resident in the main towns, small bodies of troops, military highways, a good postal service, and most important of all, regular displays of force. Local rulers were confirmed in power, but their children were often sent to Egypt — in part to be educated, in part to act as hostages for their parents' good behavior.

Misbehavior, in the sense of attempts to defy Egyptian hegemony, was the inevitable reaction to periods of apparent Egyptian sloth. Under its female sun, Hashepsowe, Egypt had attempted to turn inward; its major military intervention had been a brief raid into Nubia. Just as Tuthmosis took over, a rebellion broke out at the northern limits of Egyptian influence, along the Syrian river Orontes.

The leader of that rebellion was the prince of Kadesh, a city standing where the Bekaa valley widens into Syria. The prince of Kadesh had as his chief ally the prince of Megiddo in northern Palestine. Tuthmosis personally led an expedition against the rebel coalition. Leaving Egypt near what is now El Kantara on the Suez Canal, the monarch's forces traversed Sinai in only ten days. Another eleven days of forced march carried the Egyptian army from Gaza up the coast to the Carmel range. There Tuthmosis chose the bolder of two courses. Instead of the flatter, circuitous route proposed by his generals, he opted for the direct approach. This meant taking a narrow pass into the plain of Megiddo, that vital turntable which the author of the Book of Revelation would later choose as the site of Armageddon. Tuthmosis was astonishingly lucky, for no attempt was made to ambush the Egyptian soldiers as, over a twenty-four-hour period, they defiled through the pass. The king believed that his divine father, Amen-Re, had blinded the Asiatic rebels.

Before the decisive battle was fought on the plain, Tuthmosis arrayed himself in the insignia of godhead, appearing in a triple theophany as Horus, Amen-Re, and the second Theban deity, Montu. His victory was overwhelming; one thousand chariots were captured. Only the shortsightedness of immature troops greedy for booty prevented the immediate capture of Megiddo. But the Egyptians did arrive in time to confiscate the spring harvest, and after a grim siege lasting through the heat of summer the city surrendered in December. Tuthmosis proved as magnanimous in victory as he had been skilled in battle: there was no mass execution of princes or their sons. The hegemony that he established in this vital area lasted for a century.

The Two Lands were profoundly affected by their new close ties with western Asia. "This was an agricultural and pastoral area," one of the most perceptive historians of ancient Egypt, John A. Wilson, has written, "but it had a craftsmanship of high quality. That craftsmanship pouring into Egypt through the activity of empire was to have a profound influence upon the static calm of Egyptian art. The next century was to see more change in Egyptian artistic expression than

the preceding ten centuries." The Empire style was to be distinguished by a love of size combined with an enthusiasm for intricate detail that was almost rococo.

Tuthmosis, hardly less interested in building than his aunt Hashepsowe, gave particular attention to the temple of Amen-Re, the god whom he believed had been responsible for his victories.

Amen had long been the local god of Thebes. He was identified with the ram and still more anciently with the goose. But this animal-god had deeper resonances. The meaning of Amen was "hidden," and thanks to the instinctive process whereby the Egyptians sought for the one behind the many, he became regarded as the invisible force of the sun, and therefore truly universal. His name was linked with Re, the chief deity of the pyramid builders. Sculpted as a radiantly handsome man in a high-plumed headdress, he became the chief god of imperial Egypt. Unlike Zeus, with whom the later Greeks identified him, he was a god without scandals and was the focus of genuine piety. Many surviving prayers testify that he answered the appeals of the poor as swiftly as those of the strong. But in a worldly sense, as the proprietor of the world's largest temple, Amen-Re was the richest god in history.

The chief wonder of his temple was the Hypostyle Hall — a forest of 134 columns, some so massive that a hundred men could stand on their capitals, sixty-nine feet above the earth. But this vast hall was only the dominant feature, says Leonard Cottrell, "of a building complex which would cover much of mid-Manhattan. Within the walls of the temple there would be room for St. Peter's in Rome, the Milan Cathedral,

and Notre Dame in Paris. The outer walls would comfortably enclose ten European cathedrals." The temple was constantly enlarged, embellished, and maintained from 2000 B.C. till the birth of Christ.

The statistics regarding the temple's size and longevity are no more impressive than the figures for the personnel and property directly associated with it. At its apogee in the Nineteenth Dynasty, the temple of Amen-Re employed 81,322 people; their jobs ranged from the cerebral activities of priest and administrator to the manual labor of peasant, huntsman, and boatman. In the age of the pyramids the need to maintain a mortuary complex had alienated much land to the priesthood. The needs of the "Hidden God" accelerated this process. His shrine enjoyed the revenues of 433 gardens, 924 square miles of fields, numerous shipping yards, and whole market towns.

East-bank Thebes (today Luxor and Karnak) formed a unified city in which the division between secular and sacred was imperceptible; it was as though Versailles had been nine-tenths church and one-tenth palace. That unity was reflected in the term first used in reference to Tuthmosis III and later, thanks to the Bible, used as a generic term for every Egyptian king. The word "pharaoh" derives from the two Egyptian sounds meaning "great house." To speak of "the great house" instead of the king within it was rather like speaking of "the White House" instead of "the president." It reflects the increasing importance of officials and advisers. An empire needed a growing body of such assistants, chief among them the High Priest of Amen-Re, the Viziers of Upper and Lower Egypt, and the Viceroy of Nubia.

To us, looking at the sweep of Egyptian history from outside, the Eighteenth Dynasty may seem one bright chapter, or page. To those inside Egyptian history it lasted long enough to seem eternal. During their 250 years of rule the Eighteenth Dynasty pharaohs may have felt that they had defeated time as well as the Hyksos by reestablishing *maat*, the Egyptian concept of order and justice. In upholding *maat*, the priests were the pharaoh's delegates. Ritually clean, shaven of all body hair down to their eyelashes, they daily fed and clothed the facets of deity in dark, inmost shrines. Religious practice upheld the world's pivot — yet forces that would make this pivot wobble were at work within and without.

The essential element of the Egyptian miracle — the element that supported the pivot — was the self-confidence that had tamed the Nile, built the pyramids, and created a complex remedy even for death. This self-confidence was undermined when contact with foreigners became a daily occurrence, for western Asia was a source of doubt as well as stimulus. The military roads of Tuthmosis III thundered with chariots carrying messages written in Akkadian, the cuneiform language of Bronze Age diplomacy. The harbors of the Nile were thronged with ships importing the commodities that Egypt needed, copper from Cyprus and timber from Lebanon, and shipping out artifacts and gold. While an energetic Tuthmosis occupied the throne, while no rival empire united the squabbling statelets of the Levant in effective opposition to Egypt, such contacts with the outside world need not undermine Egyptian certainty. But if a feeble or inward-looking pharaoh were to be confronted by a foreign

A large proportion of the gold and tribute from Tuthmosis III's foreign campaigns was earmarked for the temple of Amen-Re at Karnak. The pharaoh considerably enlarged the temple by adding pylons, obelisks, and porticoes. The twin granite columns at left — embellished with the lotus and papyrus symbols of Upper and Lower Egypt, respectively — supported the roof of a hall of records devoted to Tuthmosis' military prowess. The most astounding structure in the temple complex, the Hypostyle Hall (below), was completed in the Nineteenth Dynasty by Ramesses II. Today most of its massive papyrus columns, sixty-nine feet high, stand exposed to the sky.

power capable of inflicting defeats, then Egypt would be shaken to its entrails. The decline of Egypt would take many centuries, but it could hardly be postponed.

This historical inevitability did not prevent one pharaoh from thinking up a solution that is fascinating to ponder even though it failed to arrest Egyptian decline. The heir of Amenhotep III and Queen Tiye assumed the throne in 1379 B.C. under his father's name, but then abruptly renamed himself Akhenaten. On the new king's orders the name of the god Amen-Re was deleted from most monuments. At the same time the pharaoh moved his residence from Thebes to a new, hastily built capital some three hundred miles to the north. The site, a half-moon-shaped plain on the east bank of the Nile, had been visited by Akhenaten's grandfather Tuthmosis IV. The new capital, with its sunlit, open temple to the Aten, was an attempt at Utopia and was given the name Akhetaten, or Horizon-of-the-Aten. (The site's modern name, Tell el-Amarna, comes from the names of two nearby Arab villages. See map, page 19.) The city was not without an economic base, since all the river-borne transport headed north and east passed by it and could be milked to the disadvantage of rival Thebes.

After seventeen years, first as coregent and then as sole ruler — his considerable reign testifies to a certain toughness in his personality — Akhenaten was to follow his ancestress Hashepsowe down the "memory chute." His names and titles were deleted, and his statues were pulled down and used as rubble during the reign of Ramesses II. His body was probably dismembered and burned. But since his resuscitation by modern Egyptologists he has become the most discussed

individual in the course of ancient Egypt's three thousand years and thirty dynasties. A favorite subject for the historical novelist, he has been portrayed in conflicting ways: as idealist, sexual pervert, reactionary, heretic, monster, revolutionary, and complacent smiler upon Egypt's doom. He has been accorded the qualities of a Gandhi, a Lenin, and a Marie Antoinette.

Early in Akhenaten's reign giant statues of the king were erected at Thebes to act as caryatids for an Aten chapel attached to the main temple. These images survived — through being used later to stuff one of the giant doorways, or pylons, that were a feature of Amen-Re's temple. Grotesque but haunting, they give us a vivid notion of this eccentric ruler's appearance. They show a thin-boned male with huge, protuberant belly, soft flesh, and a full-lipped sensuous face with an epicene expression; the pharaoh's eyes are charged with determined egoism.

The statues are a total break with tradition. Previously, the Egyptian artist had sculpted or painted his ruler less as he appeared to the studio eye than as he ought to appear to the eye of faith. The artist aimed at abstracting the majesty of the pharaoh from mortal man. This idealizing tendency had not prevented sculptors of genius from bequeathing us individuals: the overweight official known as the Sheikh el-Beled; the dwarf Seneb, squatting cross-legged with his wife and two children; and the tough Twelfth Dynasty pharaoh Amenhemet III, shown with a mouth supercilious, sensitive, and cruel. But no royal statue had hitherto shown natural defects or abnormalities.

If Hashepsowe was a female who pretended to be a male, Akhenaten was a male who deferred to the female in himself. He did this because to him *maat* involved fidelity to fact as much as to justice and order. This conception enhanced a theory of art which can be called naturalistic; its results combine fluidity of line and impressionistic speed of drawing with flimsy materials. When dealing with someone as authentically beautiful as Akhenaten's wife, Nefertiti, or perhaps with a kingfisher diving into sedge, Akhenaten's artists achieved a freshness not only new in Egyptian art but able to captivate future generations.

Before considering Akhenaten's other new beliefs, it is prudent to weigh the respects in which he stayed within the traditions, for his innovations grew in a traditional soil. Throughout his life he sincerely believed in his own divinity. Indeed, in his acceptance of his spiritual relationship to heaven, in his affirmation of himself as mediator between his people and the godhead, he was closer to the rulers of the Old Kingdom than to his earthly father, the pleasure-loving Amenhotep III. This conservative aspect of Akhenaten's beliefs is obscured by his tendency to push things to their limits. Because — he seems to have argued with self-centered logic — Akhenaten, as pharaoh, was a living god, nothing he did could be trivial. All his actions were of equal significance. He was not content to have himself portrayed only as warrior, huntsman, or sphinx — although he was indeed portrayed in such traditional ways. Since all he did was done by a god, his most intimate actions — fondling one of his six daughters, eating, driving with Nefertiti in a carriage, embracing his son-in-law and half brother Smenkhare, waving from a balcony — became permissible themes of art. But even these apparent innovations only push

The naturalistic mode of artistic expression that characterized
Akhenaten's reign — known as the Amarna style (from
Tell el-Amarna, the modern name of the site of the king's
capital) — had its roots in older trends. Although the official
tradition of royal portraiture decreed that the pharaoh appear
as a perfect physical and spiritual specimen, no such limitations
had been placed on earlier portrayals of private citizens and
lesser noblemen. The rotund torso and benign features of the
wooden statue at left belong to the Sheikh el-Beled, a worldly
individual who has plainly savored the profits gained from his
position as a Fifth Dynasty official. And, as early as the Sixth
Dynasty, Egyptian artists had begun to depict physical deformity:
an affecting painted limestone group statue (above left) shows the
dwarf Seneb, who was head of the royal textile works, seated
beside his sweetly smiling wife. The figures of their son and
daughter occupy the space that Seneb's lower limbs cannot fill.
A tentative groping toward realism, even in the representation of
the pharaoh, can be seen in a Twelfth Dynasty black granite
statue of Amenhemet III (above right). The figure, wearing the
conventional kilt and headdress, is posed in a rigidly orthodox
fashion, yet the modeling of the head clearly reveals the king's
forceful personality. His unusually large ears, deep-set eyes, and
dour expression form a constellation of physical attributes
as distinct as the anatomical peculiarities of Akhenaten and his
family. The unfinished quartzite head at right is a portrait of
Akhenaten's queen, Nefertiti. The construction lines are still
visible, as is the burred base to which a wig and headdress would
have been attached. By preserving for posterity the melancholy
beauty of Nefertiti's face, the unknown sculptor has fully
justified the Amarna belief in truthful representation.

to an extreme the ancient belief that the ruler is the bridge between man and god.

His political reforms seem to have combined policy, egoism, and magic. Policy: he planned to rescue the Egyptians from their dependence on an army and a priesthood by making of himself a charismatic focus, a new Cheops to unite the state. Egoism: he imagined that the new pattern, his pattern, would survive his death, that men would then continue to pray to him for admission to the afterworld. Magic: he hoped that by establishing the perfect pivot in the Horizon-of-the-Aten, his new capital, the forces of attack from outside would be stilled. Unanswered letters in the cuneiform archives show Egypt's Asian clients pleading in vain for the pharaoh to awaken from this dream.

Akhenaten's lasting fame derives from his role as a religious revolutionary. Again, what is genuinely new needs to be carefully distinguished from what is the old revived. The search for one cosmic diamond was, as we have seen, neither novel nor un-Egyptian. Ptah of Memphis and Re of Heliopolis were claimed by their devotees to be the original Word from which all else, including the other gods, descended. Even Amen-Re, the god for whom Akhenaten seems to have had a personal loathing, was identified with such an absolute. In choosing the Aten as the primal deity Akhenaten was not even particularly spiritual. It has been argued by the late Margaret Murray that the Aten, or sun disk, is less "spiritual" than Re, which is the sun at its most abstract. Nor was the choice of the Aten original: Akhenaten's grandfather had chosen the disk as the patron for his army. Moreover, his parents had maintained a barge named *The Aten Gleams* on an artificial

lake west of the Nile at Thebes (a lake that Amenhotep III had ordered completed in a fortnight to give Queen Tiye pleasure).

What was original was Akhenaten's passionate insistence that the Aten, and the Aten alone, should be worshiped. In this there is indeed a foretaste of biblical exclusiveness. We know from a stele erected during Tutankhamen's brief reign that Akhenaten carried his views into practice. The temples of other gods fell into neglect: "their shrines had become desolate and had become overgrown mounds."

Akhenaten's revolution was naturally resisted by the priestly caste, whose interests he had harmed — but its failure to establish roots doubtless sprang from his failure to convince his people. The king's enemies were silent but numerous. The measures against Amen-Re must have affected hundreds of thousands of Egyptians, all those connected to the vast caste of uncelibate priests. They must have waited impatiently for the pharaoh's abnormal physique to collapse in death.

Military men, conscious of the dangers threatening the empire, must also have sighed with relief when Akhenaten and his half brother Smenkhare were succeeded by another half brother, Tutankhaten. Although married to one of Akhenaten's daughters, Tutankhaten willingly rejected Aten-worship and changed his name back to Tutankhamen. He died at eighteen after a short reign and was buried in a modest tomb in the Valley of the Kings. With him were interred insignia embodying motifs from both cults, that of the Aten and that of Amen-Re. The men who supervised his burial laid with him one highly symbolic object: a dagger made of iron. This new metal was

smelted by the Hittites in Anatolia. Egypt had been
supreme while copper and its alloy bronze were the
dominant metals. In an age of iron she was to fare
less well.

Even so, the Atenist revolution might have left
more trace if Akhenaten's personality or ideas had
been able to inspire ordinary Egyptians. But as a man
Akhenaten was not at all the type to arouse the admiration of a deeply nationalistic and conservative people.
His physique was a caricature of his family's frailties —
the result of generations of inbreeding. The slight
build and prominent nose characteristic even of such
heroic kings as Tuthmosis III had turned into a melon-
shaped head, a scraggy neck, and unmuscular limbs.

Nor was Akhenaten's behavior pleasing to the people.
While those who saw her must have admired the
beauty of Nefertiti, they can only have deplored their
ruler's apparent subjection to a feminist court. The
father of numerous daughters but no sons, the pharaoh
was sculpted in the traditional stance of a woman, with
feet together, while his women adopted the primordial
male posture, with one foot before the other. By living
in remote Akhetaten, by swearing never to leave its
limits, he cut himself off from Egypt. The only people
who came in contact with him were his parvenu court,
his artists, the servants who brought him victuals, and
the seamen whose ships docked at the city's wharfs.

Most decisive of all, Akhenaten's cult of the Aten
brought little consolation to ordinary men and women.
Its icons showed the sun disk lowering little hands of
blessing, not on them, but on Akhenaten and his
family. The cult could be summed up as a parody of
Milton's famous line: He to love God only; us to love

God through him. Akhenaten's *Hymn to the Aten,* which has survived through having been inscribed on courtiers' tombs, struck a note both passive and remote from mundane Egyptian concerns. In Wordsworthian exaltation of the sun, the hymn made no reference to its burning heat, the aspect known to the peasant bent over the field or the quarryman working granite in the 110 degrees of an Aswan spring. The cult also struck at the major spiritual influence on ordinary Egyptians, and their greatest source of hope. Akhenaten's open attack on Amen-Re covertly attacked Osiris as well. Akhenaten and his nobles deliberately located their tombs on the east bank, not on the western horizon, traditionally sacred to the god of the afterworld. There were no representations of Osiris in the tombs — the dead were obliged to place their hopes for immortality in their eccentric pharaoh.

The real force behind the religious counter-revolution was therefore Osiris. He triumphed because his cult represented, within the autocratic system of pharaonic Egypt, a secret and compensatory democratization of the spirit. The god who had been "at the head of the stair" since the beginning of remembered times, who had died and been born again, who symbolized harvest and fertility, was the powerful comforter of Egyptians. His power and influence over ancient Egyptian society is seen in the vastly expanded use of the funerary texts that had originally been inscribed on the inner walls of the Fifth Dynasty pyramids — texts that had become powerful spells for the thousands who could afford to be buried with copies of them.

The Book of the Dead is the European title for an unstandardized collection of spells, formulae, and prayers. Their Egyptian name is more accurate: *Chapters of the Coming Forth by Day.* For as with other instances of Egyptian artistic achievement, these important texts had a strictly practical purpose: among other things they enabled the dead to leave their tombs by day and retaste the joys of life. The scribes who produced the papyrus copies of these texts often embellished them with illustrations, or vignettes, that are comparable to the finest medieval illuminations.

The *Chapters of the Coming Forth by Day* vividly reveal the character and aspirations of these long-dead people. They clearly demonstrate the Egyptians' attachment to physical life, and their hodgepodge nature illustrates a conservative refusal to throw anything away, even if this involves what to us seems a contradiction. Thus primeval spells against snakes and scorpions, and bizarre visions of the sun's journey through the underworld, coexist with lofty ideas of moral purification and judgment. Basic to these is one idea of breathtaking audacity: that ordinary man, by dying and partaking of the same mortuary rites as the god Osiris, becomes Osiris, is reborn as a god. The whole process has been described by an authority on the Theban recension of the *Chapters* as "the solarization of the dead." The mortal who took the *Chapters* with him to the grave became, like the pharaoh of old, one with the sun.

This spiritual democratization made Akhenaten's pharaoh-centered ideas seem reactionary, particularly to Egyptians uneasily aware that their status was threatened by the exigencies of empire. For a new military and political system was developing that would ultimately reduce their dignity and freedom. When power-

ful, the empire was ruled by grandiose tyrants such as Seti I and Ramesses II of the Nineteenth Dynasty, self-advertisers on a monumental scale. When weakened by Assyria and Persia, and later by Greece and Rome, a conquered Egypt would be ruled by tyrants of a foreign race.

This slow deterioration of their position attached the Egyptians more firmly than ever to the god of the afterworld. It was a changing attachment, reflected in a change of artistic styles. Until the Nineteenth Dynasty, life was probably pleasant for most Egyptians much of the time; hence in their mortuary art they attempted to charm death by vivid representations of physical life. Dancing girls, singing reapers, sailors reaching port, hunters chasing game — such images of a delightful, even joyous mortality are among the images of eternity as well.

As Egyptians became entangled in the power struggles of the Middle East, their art changed. It became gloomily obsessed with death, with mummification, and with post-mortem trials. The underworld and its denizens are shown in lurid carmine and black. According to historian John A. Wilson, this joyous and talkative people with "no more fear of death than the fear of walking in a familiar place in the dark" developed into a taciturn, gloomy people whose lot in this world was so grim that every effort, every puritan sacrifice was worthwhile in order to secure something more pleasant in the life to come. It was no longer a question of eternalizing the joyful moment. The aim was to escape from momentary toils to an eternal improvement, at whatever price in austerity and self-control.

V

Twilight of the Pharaohs

In its long and mortal disease, Egypt learned too late that foreign mercenaries represent a short-term tonic and a long-term poison. Once hirelings find their way into the barracks and then the palace, it is but a step to their taking over. What imperial Rome later experienced from German praetorians, or medieval Islam from its Turkish Mamelukes, Egypt experienced from the Greeks.

Since early in their history Greeks had been finding their way to Egypt. The seafarers of Crete and Mycenaean Greece knew that to the south, across dark, glittering waves, lay an immeasurably rich and ancient culture. In the prime work of Greek literature, the epic poems of Homer, names were mentioned that later voyagers equated with what they found in Egypt. "There is an island in the surging sea, which they call Pharos, lying off Egypt," Homer wrote. "It has a harbor with good anchorage, and hence they put out to sea after drawing water." Besides mentioning the nucleus of what would one day be Alexandria, Homer spoke of "hundred-gated Thebes." Such a city could only be the southern Egyptian capital with its many pylons — and so the metropolis known in Egyptian as Waset became Thebes for the Greeks and the West. Greeks also gave names to Egyptian things: *obelisks,* because these sun-symbols resembled little spits; *pyramids,* because they were shaped like wheaten cakes. The Greek visitors took back with them recognizable cultural influences. For example, archaic Greek statues show young men standing with one foot before another in the stiff Egyptian manner.

Only the earliest Greeks knew an Egypt still independent. Around 1100 B.C. an eleventh Ramesses had

ended the Twentieth Dynasty and Egypt had fallen under the rule of first Libyan, then Nubian rulers. The latter had proven unable to defend Egypt against the aggressive new empire of Assyria. Instead, in a shadowy paraphrase of what had happened under the Hyksos, a last vigorous dynasty, the Twenty-sixth, managed to reestablish, with the help of Greek mercenaries, a phase of independent power. This Saite dynasty, so named from its delta capital of Saïs, labored to restore the artistic and religious heritage of the Old Kingdom. Looted pyramids and tombs were piously resealed. Sculptors were commanded to labor in the ancient style, and their reproductions were remarkably fine, being sometimes hard to distinguish from the real thing. But although testifying to the reserves of talent still latent in Egyptians, Saite art tells another story — for the wish to revive former artistic modes is rarely a sign of artistic vigor. Although it is true that Victorian railway builders sponsored a neo-Gothic revival, nineteenth-century Europe was pioneering new forms of power. Saite Egypt, on the other hand, was living in a world where the balance of power and technology had moved against it.

Efforts at reviving the Egyptian empire wilted ignominiously each time they were exposed to the sun. And reconstruction of the waterway that purportedly linked Memphis to the Gulf of Suez during the Eighteenth Dynasty — and thus provided communication between the Mediterranean and the Red Sea — only made Egypt a more tempting prize. The revival of ancient power was finally proved a sham when, in 525 B.C., the Persian Great King Cambyses invaded and conquered Egypt. His successor, the talented Darius (521–486 B.C.), was to

A curious statue of Caracalla, found in Egypt, portrays the curly-haired third-century-A.D. Roman emperor in the traditional pharaonic headdress.

make some Greeks as well as all Egyptians subjects of a vast empire ruled from the Persian plateau.

Herodotus was one such subject of the Great King. His home town of Halicarnassus in southwest Anatolia (modern Turkey) was as much under Persian rule as was Egypt. Yet there was an important psychological difference between being an Egyptian vassal of Persia and a Greek one, for a Greek living in the eastern Aegean looked across an island-studded sea to independent Athens, not captive Thebes. Herodotus had been a small child when a Greek fleet at Salamis defeated the last serious Persian attempt to subjugate mainland Greece. He was a spiritual citizen of Hellas in its golden age, a contemporary of the Greek tragedians, of Pericles the democrat and of Socrates the questioning philosopher.

Herodotus, the product of this new Greek culture, visited Egypt in the middle of the fifth century. At the time of his visit, which probably lasted no more than three months, the country was temporarily in successful rebellion against Persia. What he saw and heard fills the second book of his *History,* whose main theme is the conflict between Greeks and Persians. His account is sympathetic, for the ancient country appealed to his Greek fondness for the mysterious and the spectacular. The most rational people of antiquity had a hunger for the spooky, the dark, and the new, and Herodotus found in Egypt much to satisfy such cravings in himself and his readers:

They are religious to excess, far beyond any other race of men, and use the following ceremonies — They drink out of brazen cups, which they scour every day:

there is no exception to this practice. They wear linen garments, which they are specially careful to have always freshly washed. They practise circumcision for the sake of cleanliness, considering it better to be cleanly than comely. The priests shave the whole body every other day, that no lice or other impure thing may adhere to them when they are engaged in the service of the gods. Their dress is entirely of linen, and their shoes of the papyrus plant: it is not lawful for them to wear either dress or shoes of any other material. They bathe twice every day in cold water, and twice each night; besides which they observe, so to speak, thousands of ceremonies.

Like other visitors, the Greek historian was fascinated by Egyptian mortuary habits:

The mode of embalming, according to the most perfect process, is the following: They take first a crooked piece of iron, and with it draw out the brain through the nostrils, thus getting rid of a portion, while the skull is cleared of the rest by rinsing with drugs; next they make a cut along the flank with a sharp Ethiopian stone, and take out the whole contents of the abdomen, which they then cleanse, washing it thoroughly with palm wine, and again frequently with an infusion of pounded aromatics. After this they fill the cavity with the purest bruised myrrh, with cassia, and every other sort of spicery, except frankincense, and sew up the opening. Then the body is placed in natrium for seventy days, and covered entirely over. After the expiration of that space of time, which must not be exceeded, the body is washed, and wrapped round, from head to foot, with bandages of fine linen

cloth, smeared over with gum, which is used generally by the Egyptians instead of glue, and in this state it is given back to the relations, who enclose it in a wooden case which they have made for the purpose, shaped into the figure of a man.

Herodotus gazed through eyes that were often distorted by misconceptions. For example he was convinced, without historical justification, that the Greeks had derived their gods from Egypt. He thus initiated the attempt — prolonged by others — to identify Horus with Apollo, Hathor with Aphrodite, and Amen-Re with Zeus. He had little conception that the ossified society he saw had once been innovatory, unrepetitive, and alive. He was uncritical in his acceptance of the dragomans' tales. These were not so much lies as myths (in the useful sense employed with regard to the Bible by Martin Buber) through which a people expressed their sense of the past. The legend of Cheops's tyranny in building his pyramid probably reflects contemporary Egyptian experience with their rulers. The allied legend that Cheops had closed all the temples may have been a transposed memory of the religious revolution under Akhenaten.

Herodotus possessed an eye for detail and an inquisitive mind that makes his prose a delight to read. These qualities alone would have been enough to ensure the survival of his work. But an additional preservative was his uniqueness, and because no one of comparable talent supplemented his picture, it long dominated Western appreciation of Egypt. Other possible sources were less detailed reports by later Greeks and Romans, the Hebrew scriptures, and Egyptian documents and

inscriptions. What little subsequent classical writers added to Herodotus, they added when Egypt was much further in its decline.

The Bible's attitude to Egypt is mythic, in the sense already noted. The Exodus from an Egypt plagued by Jehovah synthesizes the repeated experiences of the Bedouin peoples living on the eastern edge of Egypt. When Egypt was weak these Bedouins migrated into the delta; when Egypt was strong they were chased out again. The Golden Calf was probably a memory of Hathor, cow-eyed goddess of love; Moses is probably a pharaonic, not a Hebrew name. The most accurate sources of information would have been Egyptian inscriptions and documents. The walls of temples were embellished with hieroglyphs, while the temple libraries contained papyrus rolls written in the cursive form of the hieroglyphic script that Herodotus called "hieratic." But this complex way of writing was a priestly science rather than the plain medium for daily communication. The secret was to die out in Roman times and Egyptian records were to be unintelligible for more than fifteen centuries.

Despite their inaccuracies, the writings of Herodotus helped to familiarize his countrymen with the Nile valley and delta. So did the experiences of a growing number of veterans who settled in Egypt and traders who opened stores there. But the man destined to take over both barracks and palace was Alexander the Great, a Macedonian from the Hellenic fringe. As a Macedonian, he lacked the sceptical, rationalist temper of the Athenians. As a pupil of Aristotle, who had been a disciple of Plato, he must have heard about that conservative philosopher's visit to Egypt and his

conversations with the priests of Heliopolis. The autocratic majesty of Egyptian monarchy and the Egyptian reverence for the past had impressed Plato. In one of his dialogues he quotes an Egyptian as saying: "There is nothing beautiful nor great nor remarkable done, be it in your country or here, or in another country known to us, which has not long since been consigned to writing and preserved in our temples." Alexander was thus prepared by temperament and education for an encounter with Egypt.

He led his army into the Two Lands in 332 B.C., after defeating the Persians at the battle of Issus. Far from resisting, the Egyptians were prepared to accept him as a liberator. After visiting Memphis, Alexander went as a pilgrim to the oracular shrine of Amen-Re at Siwa, an oasis on the northern edge of the Libyan Desert. There Amen-Re, whom Alexander recognized as Zeus, purportedly recognized Alexander as his son. Alexander took this as seriously as did his new subjects. The superstitious Macedonian found it possible to balance his important earthly paternity, as son of the King of Macedonia, with an immortal paternity as son of Amen-Re. He was adapting himself to a tradition old in the time of Queen Hashepsowe, more than a thousand years before. Wearing the ram's horns in his curly hair, Alexander was acclaimed pharaoh by the Egyptians. They needed a strong pharaoh, and the handsome Greek conqueror was preferable to a Persian one.

The most durable achievement of Alexander's year in Egypt was his foundation of a new capital named after himself. Compared with all previous Egyptian capitals — Memphis and Thebes, Akhetaten and Saïs —

Alexandria embodied a new orientation, or more correctly, an occidentation. The city's two great harbors were linked to the West by the Mediterranean, and the city was severed from Egypt proper by the fresh-water lake of Maraeotis. It was also a new kind of city whose pattern of colonnaded streets, the chief of them two hundred feet wide, foreshadowed imperial Rome and even Manhattan. Despite religious ceremonies notorious for debauch, the city was primarily dedicated to the commerce, arts, and sciences of man, not to the cult of the gods. It was an Egyptian capital in which foreigners outnumbered Egyptians at least two to one.

Alexander did not live to enjoy the cool breezes and cultivated talk that were features of the new city. A year after the conquest Alexander returned to Syria to confront the Persians — and soon after subduing Darius's empire the thirty-three-year-old conqueror contracted a mysterious fever and died. One of Alexander's seven bodyguards, the Macedonian Ptolemaeus, by securing the hero's corpse and conveying it from Iraq to a central tomb, or *soma*, near the intersection of Alexandria's two main streets, helped to confirm his control over Egypt during the subdividing of Alexander's empire.

In a sense, Ptolemaeus was the founder of a thirty-first dynasty, which lasted through sixteen Ptolemies and seven Cleopatras. The members of this Macedonian family ruled as pharaohs, wearing the ancient crown and uraeus and practicing the custom, abhorrent to real Greeks, of royal incest. To bind their Greek and Egyptian subjects in one happy family they patronized a composite god, Serapis. The god's name and nature combined the two most popular Egyptian deities:

Osiris, the immemorial god of the dead, and the Apis bull, to whom Alexander had sacrificed on a visit to Memphis. This Apis cult marks the decadence of Egyptian theology. The days had gone when animals and birds were merely manifestations of the cosmic diamond; now a particular, living bull, chosen by certain signs on the death of his predecessor, was worshiped in his lifetime and after death was entombed in an underground complex of tunnels at Sakkara known as the Serapeum. In appearance Serapis was in the Greek tradition: a sceptered Zeus-like figure whose long, curly locks supported a basket containing god-knew-what mysteries.

But despite the imposing Serapeum in which this synthetic god was worshiped, despite temples in his honor as far afield as Britain and Italy, it is doubtful if Serapis united the Greeks and Egyptians. Although some Egyptians undoubtedly became Hellenized and many Greeks adopted Egyptian mystery cults and funerary habits, Alexandria remained a physically and spiritually divided city.

Physically, the city's nucleus was the islet mentioned by Homer and now joined by a T-shaped causeway to a longer limestone reef running from the fishing village known as Rhakotis in the west to near the outlet of the Nile's Canopic mouth to the east. The central portion of the town, at the base of the T, belonged to the Greeks, whose marble and pillars set the style for the most lavish public buildings the world had yet seen. Beyond the royal palace on the horn of the eastern harbor stretched a large and prosperous Jewish quarter, the biggest concentration of Jews outside the Holy Land. Rhakotis was the Egyptian quarter.

For a thousand years the Greeks were to dominate Alexandria and Egypt, either directly during the three Ptolemaic centuries or indirectly under the Roman empire and its Byzantine successor. Greek was the language of government, taxation, and commerce. The building that symbolized Ptolemaic Alexandria took its name from Homer's island: the Pharos, a gigantic lighthouse, rose to a height of four hundred feet and was surmounted by a great polished mirror of steel lit by beacons. In being gigantic, the Pharos was in the Egyptian tradition; in being dedicated to a secular purpose — the guidance of seafarers into the city's two harbors — it was Hellenic. For the Ptolemies, despite their acceptance of pharaonic costumes and customs, promoted an essentially humanist culture. Alexandria could never rival Athens, focus of the Greek golden age, for even at their early best the Ptolemies were despots; they could never offer scholars the groves of Akademe, since these had been defoliated by the very victories that had given these despots their power.

Alexandria was the focus of a silver age, but even so it was an age that witnessed important contributions to the arts and sciences. The nautical lighthouse had its cultural counterpart in the great Library and Mouseion that the Ptolemies built south of their own seaside palace. In reigns spanning a century, the first three Ptolemies attracted leading Greek scholars to their capital. With royal cooperation these scholars established the ancient world's largest collection of books written on papyrus, ultimately comprising something close to half a million volumes. Legend has it that Ptolemy II confined seventy-two rabbis in seventy-two huts on the island of Pharos and that these men produced identical versions of the Septuagint, the first Greek translation of the Hebrew scriptures. The same Ptolemy sponsored a history of Egypt written in Greek by Manetho, an Egyptian priest. Manetho's work, which survives in quotations, particularly in the work of the Jewish historian Josephus, gives us our classification of Egyptian rulers into thirty dynasties.

The Mouseion was an original establishment that foreshadowed a modern university in many ways. Royal subsidies enabled scholars from all over the Greek world to live, study, and lecture in its congenial environment. Among the most memorable of its literary figures were: Callimachus, poet-librarian under Ptolemy II; Apollonius Rhodius, author of a scholarly epic, *Argonautica*; and the best of all, Theocritus, the first urban author of pastorals. Alexandria was particularly rich in grammarians, critics, and lexicographers — and while it is difficult to enthuse over pedants, we owe them the accurate survival of the more creative poets and prose writers of an earlier age.

The Alexandrian contribution to the sciences was remarkable. Euclid not only founded Alexandria's mathematical school, but the tradition that has led to modern technology. When Ptolemy I asked Euclid if there were no shorter road to mastering his *Elements* — a question echoed later by generations of schoolboys — the mild scientist answered: "There is, alas!, no *royal* road to geometry." The flat Egyptian landscape with its geometrical pyramids may well have inspired geometry's pioneer.

Another Greek scientist undoubtedly aided by Egypt's topography was Eratosthenes, successor to Callimachus as chief librarian and the first man in history

to measure the Earth. He did so after hearing that in midsummer the noonday sun at Aswan lit up a well to its total depth. Having satisfied himself that Aswan lay on a tropic, Eratosthenes next calculated the sun's midsummer zenith at Alexandria, five hundred miles north. Eratosthenes discovered that these five hundred miles corresponded to a fiftieth of a giant circle of approximately 25,000 miles, which he thus posited as the Earth's circumference. In calculating the Earth's diameter at 7,850 miles, he erred by only 50 miles.

If the Greeks in this cosmopolitan city left memorable legacies in art and science, the Jews who lived east of the royal palace profoundly affected the religious ideas of the entire West. The Jewish community's relations with its pagan neighbors were ambivalent, and an authority on Hellenistic culture has written, "It was perhaps in Alexandria that anti-Semitism had its beginning." The same Manetho who bequeathed us the dynastic system also posited the rather extraordinary hypothesis that the Exodus had simply been the expulsion of a section of the Egyptian people disfigured by leprosy and scrofula. Greek dislike of the Jews was occasioned by the way they held aloof from a pagan world in which everyone took part in everyone else's ceremonies and wherein no one claimed the possession of exclusive truth. The Jews at no time evidenced a readiness to incorporate Serapis in their synagogue worship, yet their dedication to one god and their scrupulous adherence to Jewish law attracted as many Alexandrians as it repelled. Educated Greeks had long found it impossible to believe in the Twelve Olympians, and later Platonic thought, though ingenious, did not satisfy them.

On the Jewish side, there was an equal ambivalence. In Palestine, particularly under the Jewish nationalist leaders known as the Maccabees, Hellenism was identified with all that was odious to God: idolatry, sensual enjoyment, and pride in physical force. But the Jews living in Alexandria had a more balanced vision of the Hellenistic world. On the one hand, they saw at even closer range the pagan pomps hated by their brethren in Jerusalem, the fleshly world symbolized in the Tanagra figurines, which show human beings as they really are. On the other hand, knowing Greek, they could appreciate the immense developments in human thought achieved by the thinkers of Hellas.

Alexandria was thus a crucible for the melting together of very different cultures. On a religious level, the more thoughtful Greeks were disposed to be influenced by Judaism; on a philosophical level, the more open-minded Jews were ready to be influenced by Hellas. The interaction took place in many ways. Greeks attended Jewish worship and found it, by comparison with the feasts of paganism, akin to the philosophic discourse in some ideal republic. Some went as far as undergoing the distasteful rite of circumcision. On their side, Jews began to open the papyrus rolls in which the thoughts of Plato and Aristotle were to be found. The Jewish community began to debate whether the whole gentile culture ought to be rejected or whether elements in it might not prove to be both admirable and useful.

The greatest Jewish synthesist was Philo, an older contemporary of Christ in good standing with the pagan authorities. In his writings Philo fused the experiences of the Hebrews, with their keen sense of the movement of God in history, and the abstract terms, lacking in Hebrew, in which the Greeks had embodied their intellectual discoveries. On some levels Philo seems merely to have accommodated what seemed uncouth in the Jewish tradition to pagan sophistication. Circumcision and restrictions on diet were explained in allegorical terms: the first symbolized the excision of evil passions while the second reminded man of ethical imperatives. But in his acceptance of the validity of the mystical experience, above all in the concept of the Logos as the intermediary factor between Creator and created, Philo left attitudes and verbal expressions of prime importance to the later development of Christianity. That the doctrine of the Logos also echoes the ancient theology of Ptah shows that Alexandria was indeed a crucible of many traditions.

But Alexandria was never a city where the Egyptians felt at home. Their unofficial capital was a new city, opposite Memphis, built where the canal leading to the Gulf of Suez diverged from the Nile. Its name, Babylon-in-Egypt, has been given two explanations. According to one, Chaldean workmen brought to Memphis from Babylon revolted against their Persian masters and established themselves on a mound on the east bank. Having been granted an amnesty, they were allowed to settle the area and name it after their home city on the Euphrates. Another explanation sees in Babylon a corruption of Bab-li-On, the Gateway to On, the ancient name for Heliopolis. Whatever its origin, Babylon-in-Egypt was the first important settlement on the site of the future Cairo. Unlike Alexandria, it was crowded, huddled, and secret. It symbolized the chasm between triumphant Hellenism and an

Egyptian culture reduced to being a poor relation in its own homeland.

Not that the Ptolemies showed outward contempt for the culture of their subjects. On the contrary, they probably prided themselves on the tolerance they showed their dark-skinned subjects, and at least to begin with, on an administration that was more just and less onerous than most. But the later Ptolemies, lacking the qualities of the first three, extracted taxes for foreign wars that exhausted the countryside or for civil wars that devastated it. Like all tax merchants, they were hated. Their scrupulous imitation of Egyptian customs seemed part of the trickery for which Greeks had been renowned since the time of Odysseus.

If the Ptolemies had persecuted the old religion, or remained contemptuously aloof from it, the Egyptians might have found in Horus and Isis standards around which to rally. But when the Egyptians entered their temples, they found the Ptolemies there, and their inscriptions. If the temples crumbled, the Ptolemies repaired them — so frequently and so well that this Macedonian dynasty ranks among the greatest builders in Egyptian history. Their shrine of Horus at Edfu and of Hathor at Dendera are two of the best-preserved temples awaiting the present-day tourist. Most of what remains of the island temple of Isis at Philae, just south of Aswan, was the result of reconstruction started by Ptolemy II (surnamed Philadelphus, or "lover of his sister") and completed by Ptolemy III (surnamed Euergetes, "doer of good works").

Instead of embracing Hellenism or preserving their ancient culture, the Egyptians took refuge in mystery cults and magic. Eloquent archaeological evidence of that decadence can be found in Ptolemaic funerary relics: scraps of paper with a few crude symbols inscribed on them replace the papyrus masterpieces that had comprised the *Chapters of the Coming Forth by Day*. In the Fayum oasis, an area of heavy foreign settlement, Greek colonists had themselves buried in anthropoid coffins, their faces simpering through eternity in painted stucco. The deep, arcane soul of the Egyptians was outraged; it waited eagerly for some new interpretation of the cosmic diamond.

Yet through lack of an alternative, the Ptolemies ruled, with diminishing effectiveness, for three hundred years — or half a century longer than the great dynasty of Hashepsowe and Tuthmosis III. The dynasty expired with Cleopatra VII in 30 B.C. Cleopatra is as much history's first Levantine as Egypt's last Horus-sovereign. "Levantine" is an unflattering adjective coined in recent centuries for someone who lives in the Middle East without belonging to it, who speaks many languages without possessing one of his own, who has decadent tastes, whose armory springs from his wits rather than his muscle, who looks to outside forces for his succor and succubus. Cleopatra was in many respects a prototype. Her name was Greek, being found in Homer; she dressed as a Greek, except when arraying herself as Isis. Her father, Ptolemy XII, surnamed the Flute-Player, had been illegitimate, and her claim to twilight Egypt, which had by now lost Cyprus, its last shred of empire, was through marriage, first to her half brother Ptolemy XIV, then after his death in battle to one still younger, Ptolemy XV.

Cleopatra spent her life watching the struggle of outside forces: first Pompey against Caesar; then the

Egypt's foreign rulers adopted and modified for their own use the ancient custom of mummification. During the first three centuries of Roman rule, a portrait of the deceased — painted in wax colors on wood — was commonly attached to the mummy wrappings of both natives and conquerors. A vast cache of these mummies, discovered at the Fayum Oasis during the nineteenth century, includes the portraits of a Greek boy and girl below. Startlingly modern in their realistic execution and luminous use of color, these expressive studies contrast sharply with the grim profile stamped on the silver denarius at right. The legendarily seductive Cleopatra, last of the Ptolemies, appears as a fleshy matron with jutting chin and prominent nose.

assassins of Caesar against his avenger, Antony; then Antony against Caesar's great-nephew, the future Augustus. When Caesar invaded Egypt, she had herself smuggled to his palace wrapped in a carpet. She accompanied him to Rome and had by him a son, whose pet name was Cesarion. Through Cesarion, or Ptolemy XVI, she continued to reign, having meanwhile poisoned her fraternal spouse, Ptolemy XV.

Cleopatra's mind was in firm control of her libido, which she used effectively to beguile first Caesar, then Antony. Her sensual imagination seems to have been untiring. Her will was insatiable and opportunistic, and although her opportunities were constricted by fate, she used them to the full. As a ruler, she was a failure, and as a military ally to Antony, a disaster. The flight of sixty Egyptian ships under Cleopatra's command from the decisive battle of Actium not only reduced Antony's fleet but, in their precipitate desire to get back to Egypt, broke his battle line.

Yet behind her ruthless, European temperament — which only the Romans of the day could have equated, as they did, with the dangerous East — was a streak of identification with her people. Although by blood she was as alien to them as such later rulers as Farouk, the Egyptians accepted Cleopatra as completely as their ancestors had accepted Hashepsowe, a full-blooded Egyptian. She, for her part, had that ability to identify with a foreign people which recurs in such later figures as Lady Hester Stanhope in Lebanon or Lafcadio Hearn in Japan.

Besides Greek and Latin, Cleopatra spoke the language of her subjects — and accepted their mythology. After she had been loved as a girl by Caesar and as a mature woman by his successor, after she had sailed in gilded barges to paltry destinations, after she had accepted as a plaything a pirate kingdom in southern Anatolia, after the game was lost and she faced a choice of defeats, she chose to die royally. Her death excited the admiration of Plutarch, and through him, Shakespeare. Plutarch, eager for examples of Hellenic heroism to set against heavy Roman virtue, tells how she chose to slay herself, not with a bare bodkin, but with the very symbol of Egyptian kingship, the cobra, or uraeus. It had reared on every pharaoh's head since Narmer's, and it now reared on hers as she held the market-woman's cobra to her naked breast.

VI
New Faith in an Ancient Land

The Roman invaders, sticklers for protocol, ruled Egypt as heirs of the Ptolemies — and in similar style. Octavian, the future Augustus, established his legal claim to the Egyptian throne in two simple stages. First, he murdered Cesarion, Cleopatra's son by Julius Caesar, Octavian's great-uncle and adoptive father; second, he declared himself Cleopatra's heir, since she had once been married to Caesar. The Egyptians accepted the claim. "The fact," Arthur Weigall notes, "that Octavian was hailed by Egyptians as King of Egypt long before he was recognized by Romans as Emperor of Rome, gave the latter throne a kind of Pharaonic origin in the eyes of the vain Egyptians."

Antony's neglected wife, Octavian's sister, looked after three of Cleopatra's children at her house in Rome. It is possible that Augustus, having secured the wealth of Egypt, might have allowed Cleopatra to grow old in exile. If, instead of suicide, she had chosen such a fate, she might well have been alive, a woman in her late sixties, when the next group of "invaders" entered Egypt.

These invaders were a refugee family from Palestine. At the El Kantara frontier post, an elderly paterfamilias, his adolescent wife, her baby, and a midwife completed the frontier formalities and entered what was by then a de facto Roman province governed by Gaius Turranius. Frightened and tired, they had followed the Sinai road taken long before them by the Hyksos, the Hebrew patriarchs, and the soldiers of Alexander. Like previous arrivals, the family from Bethlehem in Judaea must have sighed with relief at the spectacle of the vivid delta, so temptingly green after the desert. Their destination was not Hellenized Alexandria but the largely Egyptian city of Babylon-in-Egypt at the neck of the delta; that city had a small Jewish quarter.

Their route took the little party's donkeys past Heliopolis. As Jesus and his parents approached the fresh-water spring known as the Source of the Sun, there were, according to legend, prodigious happenings in this center of Re worship. Gigantic statues of Ptah the Half-mummified and Thoth the Bird-headed, of swaddled Osiris and his sister-wife Isis, crashed to the ground in spontaneous homage to incarnate truth. In Babylon, Joseph sold the gifts of the Magi — gold, frankincense, and myrrh — to finance the party's travels deep into Upper Egypt.

Like other legends, the Holy Family's sojourn in Egypt is disputed in part or in whole. But the disputable legend stands for an indisputable truth. After Cleopatra's death, Egyptians of all races seem to have stampeded away from ideas that had satisfied their ancestors. All three communities that made up Ptolemaic Alexandria — Greeks, Jews, and Egyptians — were affected. And each group produced adherents to the new faith, which preached that the infant refugee was the divine Logos in human shape. Mary's son, not Ptah or the Aten, was the primal impulse through which the world had been made; Jesus, not Osiris, was the god at the head of the stair who could confer eternal life. The Egypt that had linked delta and valley to form the world's first state would now unite Egyptian, Greek, and Hebrew elements to form Christian theology; the land in which the embalmer had held the key to eternal life would now advance the ascetic, the martyr, and the monk in his place.

The appealing, wide-eyed gaze of this small limestone statue of a saint holding a cross reflects the simple piety of the Copts, the native Egyptian Christians who suffered severe persecution under Roman rule.

Christianity first spread among the unremarked. Its roots are as lost in dust as the unmummified bodies of the poor. But its seedbed was the Jewish community. The Acts of the Apostles records the presence of Egyptian Jews in Jerusalem at the time of Pentecost; the church at Alexandria claimed to have been founded by Saint Mark. While many Jews recognized Jesus as the Messiah, others refused to accept the Incarnation and fiercely opposed the Church, persecuting and then being persecuted in return.

From its Jewish seedbed the new faith spread to Greeks, whose restless minds were disposed to welcome a new conception and were equipped to refashion it in every conceivable form. The Greeks of Alexandria, along with some Hellenized Egyptians, made decisive contributions to the dogmatic life of the new religion. These apparently willful variants and heresies were by-products of an unparalleled intellectual activity that, over some centuries, produced the creeds still shared by Catholic, Orthodox, and most Protestant Christians. The most detailed creed, the Athanasian, was the fruit of an ideological battle between two Egyptians: the victor, Athanasius, who devoted a long life to maintaining the divinity of Christ, and the heretic, Arius, who as passionately denied that the Word was coeternal with God.

The new religion had a revolutionary effect on native Egyptians. The Christian Logos, carried in the arms of a young girl on a donkey, dealt a far more drastic blow to a culture by then three thousand years old than had the armies of previous invaders, for soldiers had invariably succumbed to Egypt's imposing antiquity and self-confident culture. The Hyksos had

reigned as pharaohs in their delta capital, as had the Ptolemies in Alexandria. The Caesars were no less susceptible on visits to their Egyptian estate, arguing with the skeptical humanism of a Hadrian that there was probably more truth in these mystery cults than in Romulus and Remus. The Roman acceptance of Egyptian ways is shown in an underground necropolis for the rich discovered in Alexandria: in this pagan Forest Lawn, Anubis wears a Roman kilt while curly-haired plutocrats stand in the traditional pharaonic posture, one foot before the other.

The Holy Family was a product of Judaism's long evolution. Unlike the early Hebrews, who had been much tempted by the fleshpots of Egypt, they had a basis of conviction from which to disdain pharaonic culture and religion. The Jews, originally a tribe of nomads, had produced through the dialogue of their prophets and much painful loyalty to their Law the self-confidence of a new order. The new Word from Palestine would reduce the many words of the past — the spells and incantations of the funerary texts, the sacred writings on temple walls — to unintelligible designs that learned men of later ages would doubt had ever constituted a written language.

No conqueror, let alone no small Palestinian family, could have overthrown so vast a structure of belief, ritual, and artistic tradition if the timbers of the structure had still been sound. They were not. After thirty dynasties and the Ptolemaic kiss of death, Egyptian culture had lost its power to compel. The Egyptians of the pyramid age had worked miracles of engineering because they believed in what they were doing. Under later rulers they had repeatedly rallied to reject invaders and to reestablish their distinctive norms, for they saw these norms as manifestations of an order destined to last forever. As late as the Twenty-sixth Dynasty Egyptian artists had produced works that are sometimes hard to distinguish from those produced under the Old Kingdom. With the Ptolemies this power to compel had leaked away. Egypt was waiting for a new faith.

Christianity gave a revolutionary new answer to the perennial question of Egyptian civilization — the question to which the Great Pyramid had been the most spectacular answer, and the invention of sculpture and painting the most moving: how can a man ensure that he will continue to live with the gods after death?

The answers had developed subtly, without ever losing certain common ideas. The ordinary builders of the pyramids had associated their own immortality with that of their king, and Egyptians of later times had even dared to associate themselves with Osiris, to become Osiris So-and-So after death. Survival after death had long been linked with right action in life. The *Chapters of the Coming Forth by Day* contain a series of "negative confessions" addressed to Osiris, who was regarded as the judge of the dead, not merely their mechanical reviver. But even the most sophisticated thinkers, whether they were priests of Re or revolutionaries like Akhenaten, still attached great importance to funerary rites. Since these were not only complex but expensive, a man's chances of a blissful afterlife depended to a great extent on his being rich. The *ka* of a man too poor to have his body embalmed and coffined had a slender chance of eternal survival.

Christianity's revolutionary answer to this problem had a burning impact on Egyptians overtaxed by foreign landlords and increasingly ravaged by raiders from Nubia. Eternal life, according to the new doctrine, depended on the acceptance of Jesus as the Word who had entered into a human body, a body he had then offered as a sacrifice through which all men could escape the doom of death. It was the least costly way to heaven yet proposed. It was a way easier for the beggar than for the rich, as the parable of Dives and Lazarus showed. Immortality in no sense depended on the preservation of the cadaver. Jesus himself had spoken with sarcasm of whitewashed tombs, all splendor without and rotting ignominy within.

Christianity also offered total forgiveness of sins. This gift Egyptians found difficult to accept at face value; nothing so easy could be effective. They had an instinctive urge to work out their salvation with as much difficulty as possible, and the sterner sayings of Christ attracted them — especially those that recommended the sacrifice of a limb in preference to damnation. The Egyptians could supplement Christ's brief references to Hell with a demonology as old as the pyramids. To escape Hell, to achieve that spiritual cleanliness which mattered so much more than ritual purity, they embraced asceticism. Their fasts were longer and more frequent than those of Christians in other lands. They accepted penances as harsh as the punishments in the Roman army. They welcomed temptations more concrete than those that had bedeviled the Savior. In an extreme example of the Egyptian urge to bodily sacrifice, Origen, one of the most brilliant minds of the early church, replied to

Coptic iconography drew upon both pagan and Christian themes for inspiration. Carved in high relief on the architectural fragment below is the figure of Aphrodite, the Greek goddess of love, set against the curves of a stylized sea shell.

the temptations of the flesh by having himself castrated.

Only some Greeks had embraced Christianity; others adhered to the fashionable Neo-Platonic philosophy. To this group the fast-spreading Galilean faith seemed a peasant barbarism, and they oppressed their Christian tenants with great zeal. The sect was also harassed by the Roman government, which saw the new movement as subversive — a charge most Christians accepted without dispute. First under Decius, then under Diocletian, Christians were persecuted on a scale so vast that the church in Egypt later dated its beginning from this bloodstained period.

Asceticism, self-mutilation, even martyrdom — all involved individual sacrifice. Even more remarkable was the extent to which, on a collective level, Egyptian Christians sacrificed their historic past. While the Greeks who accepted Christianity grafted the new faith to their classical philosophy, the Egyptians cut down their ancient tree, spurning all its fruits. They abandoned hieroglyphics in favor of the Greek alphabet, taking over eight symbols from the demotic form of the old writing to represent consonants not found in Greek. Strangest of all, they began to identify themselves in myth with the Hebrews of the Old Testament: they crossed the Red Sea into the Promised Land of the heavenly kingdom, heaping curses on pharaoh and his soldiers — their own ancestors. They totally rejected their pagan past, and no aesthetic considerations stayed their hands when it came to defacing ancient monuments or putting them to a new, Christian use.

The term Coptic, used for native Egyptian Christians, can henceforth be used with convenience, although historically it came into use at a later date. The Copts, like other early Christians, believed that the end of the world was approaching, and they were not anxious to rival the grandeur of the pyramids and Sphinx. Their churches were either converted pagan shrines or basilicas on the Roman model. But the artistic urge continued to be strong. Coptic art reflects a talented and bigoted people, deeply influenced by Greek art — not the art of the golden age, but the repetitive yet insistent modes of Alexandria and the Hellenistic age. The Copts took these decadent modes and gave them a sturdy new expression, sometimes grotesque but always vital. It is a peasant expression, the art not of masters but of the oppressed. It shows an ebullient desire to communicate, whether in intricate tapestries or pathetic monuments to the dead. And it retains ghostlike links with the past: the *ankh,* or pharaonic symbol of eternal life, becomes the cross; a uraeus design appears on a Christian tomb. But for the most part this peasant art submits to the influences of Greece or the Bible. The Virgin Mary is as likely to be portrayed as Aphrodite of Cyprus as Isis of Egypt. Patriarchs of the church replace kings.

In its rough, provincial way, Coptic art heralds the more majestic art of Byzantium, but it is not the artistic legacies of Christian Egypt that are the most important. The modern world would be what it is, and only art historians would seriously suffer, if the Copts had never embroidered cloth, carved ivory, chiseled stone, or illustrated their religious texts. But the West would be profoundly different without the Coptic contribution to the machinery through which Christianity survived the collapse of the Roman empire. By invent-

ing Christian monasticism, the Copts created, inside great lowering walls, spiritual equivalents of the Pharos lighthouse. Thanks to these monks and their successors, much of man's ancient discoveries continued to shine through the dark ages of European history.

The founder of monasticism was Saint Anthony, the son of rich Christians from Upper Egypt. His parents died when he was not yet twenty, leaving him responsible for a large amount of land and a younger sister. A *Life* written by his friend Athanasius tells us that "nearly six months after, he heard read in the church those words of Christ to the rich young man: 'Go sell what thou hast, and give it to the poor, and thou shalt have treasure in heaven.' " This absolute command had already been dismissed by countless Christians as a counsel of perfection. Anthony heard it with literal-mindedness. Going home, he made over 120 acres to neighbors — to cover all future taxes for himself and his sister; the rest of his estate he sold and gave to the poor, except for what sufficed to have his sister maintained in a house of pious women. Thus freed from worldly cares he began a new life that was destined to be long (he died at 105) and uncomfortable (he dieted on bread, salt, and water, and slept on a rush-mat bed) — but also joyful ("Strangers knew him from among his disciples by the joy which was always painted on his countenance, resulting from the inward peace and composure of his soul").

For fifteen years Anthony prayed and fasted in seclusion — and because asceticism had as much appeal in the fourth century as athletics or pop music has in the twentieth, his fame spread. In order to escape attention and intensify his austerities, he moved to a

ruined tomb on the east bank of the Nile. There he was assailed by what he took to be demons but were probably the irruptions into Anthony's consciousness of his repressed desires. His crude cell attracted admirers who populated every cave and cranny in the district. When they begged him to give them a rule of life, he consented; and in a further migration moved to the bare, grassless hills by the Red Sea. From a lofty cave in those hills, Anthony superintended an ascetic community settled around a spring. From this retreat he walked to Alexandria on several occasions — on one occasion when he was over a hundred years old — to support Athanasius. When at last he felt the approach of death, he sternly ordered two disciples not to have him embalmed, although this pagan practice was still followed by some Christians. Instead, they were to bury his body secretly in the mountains. "In the day of the resurrection, I shall receive it incorruptible from the hands of Christ."

To this day Anthony's desert monastery survives behind high, Beau-Geste walls. As in the fourth century, the walls enclose a collection of individuals living separately and assembling for prayer; each of the Coptic monks has a house of his own in what amounts to a village in a walled oasis.

Anthony's monasticism was neither the first in history nor the only kind produced in Egypt; both Buddhists and Essenes had preceded him in such communal religious living. Nor was his rather individualistic form of monasticism to be the most typical. One of his friends, Pachomius, a veteran of the army of Constantine the Great, initiated a more disciplined form, imposing the severities of a sergeant-major on

The carved reliefs on Coptic tombstones reveal remnants of a pharaonic artistic heritage. An intricate pattern of lotus-form columns decorates the limestone slab at left. On the funerary steles below and at right, the hieroglyph for life, the ankh, has been transformed into a Christian cross.

monks whose barrackslike monasteries were the prototypes of later European models. The monks of Saint Pachomius engaged in agricultural work when they were not praying. The work was not designed merely to prevent evil thoughts; in the immemorial tradition of Egyptian agriculture, it was seen as valid in its own right. Saint Benedict's motto that "to work is to pray" was in the tradition of Pachomius.

During the lifetime of Anthony, Egyptian and Greek Christians, theologians and ascetics, still formed one brotherhood. The fraternal practices of early Christianity were as important as its teaching on the afterlife. Pre-Christian society had been segmented: Jew holding aloof from Greek and rich from poor, while the free man was an entirely different being from the slave. In one of his letters Saint Paul, by upbringing a strictly orthodox Jew, announced that all such differences had been dissolved in Christ. Admittedly this revolution was largely theoretical; the End was felt to be so near that it was hardly worthwhile changing more than the spirit of social relations. (Another letter shows that Paul advised a slave who had taken the message literally to return to his master.) But during the years of Roman persecution — the long decades in which the catacomb, not the cathedral, symbolized the church's position — differences of race, class, and culture melted in the heat of common peril in much the same way that World War II air raids drove duchesses and their parlor maids to the same subway shelter. With peace, such solvents stiffened — and when Christianity became the official religion of the empire in the fourth century, native Egyptians found that the baptized bureaucracy remained bureau-

cratic, that Christian tax collectors often used the whip, and that the converted Caesar in the new Rome of Constantinople was a politician before he was a Christian (which meant, in the terms of the day, that he intrigued, indulged, and tortured as if the Holy Spirit had never descended).

In Egypt, those at the receiving end of state oppression were Egyptians, while the bureaucrats and tax collectors of the Byzantine Caesars were Greeks. Thus the united church — in which Greeks expressed their genius in one way and the Egyptians in another — began to sunder. This tendency to schism was not peculiar to Egypt: all across North Africa there was a similar tendency for national differences to express themselves in schisms and heresies. The native populations showed dislike for their Byzantine rulers by supporting variants on the complex Christian creed. An oppressed group could thus manifest feelings for which the political machinery made no allowance.

The crisis for Egypt occurred in A.D. 451 when the church held its fourth ecumenical congress at Chalcedon. At this gathering of six hundred bishops, practically all of whom came from the East, the bishop of Rome claimed supremacy. This claim was resisted by the Copts, to whom the see of Alexandria was of equal rank with Rome. The Council of Chalcedon was, in Christian terms, a scandal, being a pandemonium of insult and menace whose result was a major schism destined to last until the twentieth century. The Egyptians expressed their particularity by espousing what came to be known as the Monophysite position — that Christ had only one composite nature. The position upheld by both old and new Rome was that Christ had

two natures in perfect balance. In adopting the Monophysite position, the Copts may have been instinctively reverting to their ancient view of a pharaoh, whose nature combined manhood and godhead without much difficulty.

As the Copts gathered increased support from other dissident groups in the Middle East, a rival church began to form. And when the Byzantines banished a popular, Monophysite patriarch of Alexandria, the breach became final. Later emperors were to try, unsuccessfully, to end the schism — sometimes by using force, sometimes by proposing a compromise formula, such as the theory that Christ had two natures but only one will. Such semantic bridges carried little traffic, for the argument about the nature of Christ concealed something more down to earth: the disillusion of native Egyptians with a new Christian empire so sadly resembling the old, repudiated pagan one. The schism festered until the mutual distrust of the two communities reached its climax in the early seventh century. When fire-worshiping Persians invaded the Middle East and carried off the True Cross from Jerusalem, Byzantium was proved to be as ineffective as it was oppressive. The disillusion was so great that when a new invading army, this time from Arabia, crossed Sinai in 639 to threaten Egypt, the Coptic majority watched with indifference the struggle between their Greek masters and the Arabs. They did nothing to prevent the Arabs from winning.

The Arabs were not strangers to the Copts; Arab caravans had frequently visited Babylon-in-Egypt. But the Arab army that camped just north of the walled city had changed in quality. Its soldiers behaved with

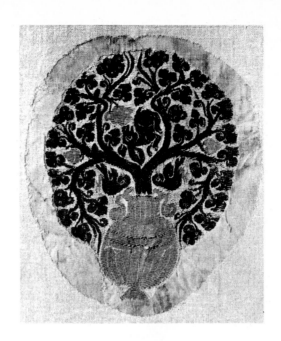

exemplary decorum and practiced a fraternal equality unseen in Christian circles for several centuries. They respected women and obeyed their commander, Amr, when he told them to treat their neighbors the Copts with all possible gentleness. The watchers from the battlements were particularly impressed when, five times a day, the whole army prostrated itself in prayer to the southeast, toward the new holy city of Mecca, while a Moslem with a stentorian voice proclaimed that there was no god but God and that Muhammad was his messenger.

Once again a new concept of God, a concept sterner but simpler to understand than that of the Christian Logos, was to win an increasing number of Egyptian converts. Islam, as the new religion was called, accepted Jesus as the spirit of God and Mary as his virgin mother; but the Koran, the scripture of the new faith, was uncompromising in its assertion that God was neither begotten nor did he beget. Jesus, like Moses and Muhammad, was a mortal messenger from God.

The conversion of Egypt to Islam would never be total and the conversion of the majority did not happen quickly, for Islam was tolerant of those who possessed some form of scripture. Jews and Christians could, if they preferred, keep their own variant of monotheism and simply pay a head tax in lieu of military service. For a considerable time the caliphs, Muhammad's successors as rulers of Islam, were content to run Egypt through a Coptic administration. The Arabs collected their head tax and shipped much of the country's vegetable wealth to barren Arabia by way of the shallow canal used during the Eighteenth Dynasty and maintained in Roman times as the "river of Trajan."

Under the Arabs, the Copts enjoyed more freedom than under the Byzantines. The best Coptic literature — all of it religious — derives from the first centuries of the caliphate.

But with the passage of time there was a steady seepage from the Christian community into Islam. This happened for several reasons. On the Islamic side, some rulers thought it meritorious to collect, instead of the head tax, a harvest of Egyptian souls. Various forms of pressure speeded the collection. They grew more severe when Islam was involved in wars with Christian Europe or Byzantium and the presence of a large Christian population in Egypt seemed a threat. On the Coptic side, some accepted Islam through genuine conversion, others through a wish to be first-class citizens in the Islamic state. But it says much for the spiritual courage of Copts as well as for the tolerance that seems part of the Egyptian climate that in the twentieth century, after more than thirteen centuries of Islamic rule, a vigorous Coptic church, sister to the state church of Ethiopia, still exists in Egypt, numbering somewhere around 10 per cent of the population. Elsewhere in North Africa — a hot littoral between desert and sea — the indigenous Christian community was to disappear, leaving only the mosaic pavements and broken pillars of its churches.

Coptic craftsmen excelled in the art of textile weaving. They adorned tunics and shrouds with plant and floral motifs, such as the carefully pruned tree at left. In the tapestry below, the sprightly figures of two disciples are poised below an ornamental flowered border.

VII
Arabs and Archaeologists

Egypt's submission, first to Arab rule and then over the centuries to the Arabian religion, represented a final lobotomy of the pharaonic past. The Copts had raged against their pagan forebears and used their temples as churches or monastic cells. The temple of Hashepsowe, to give but one example, housed a monastic community (hence its modern name of Deir el-Bahri, or the northern monastery). But even so the Copts still used a language basically the same as that of the pyramid builders, even if its grammar had changed with the centuries and its vocabulary was larded with loanwords from Greek. Such tenuous bonds were now to be severed. In becoming a province of Islam — a faith in which religion, state, and culture formed an intricate whole — Egypt became part of a new entity. Dramatic changes affected the way she was governed, the manner in which she phrased her age-old search for god, her relationship with Europe, and not least, her relationship with the human wonders that had survived to puzzle those who could no longer understand either the pharaonic writing or language. For the Egyptians who accepted Muhammad as their prophet adopted the language of the Koran — and soon even the Copts spoke Arabic. Although Coptic texts were still being written as late as the fourteenth century, Coptic ceased to be a spoken language after 1100.

The most immediate result of Amr's conquest in A.D. 641 was political. Egypt was lifted out of the Byzantine world and placed at the center of a new empire that linked the torrid regions of the globe from Morocco in the west to India and Central Asia in the east. Egypt was ruled by governors sent from a series of caliphal capitals, each representing a shift of emphasis within the Islamic world. The first such capital had been Medina, the City of the Prophet, in western Arabia. After the death of the first four caliphs, all friends and contemporaries of Muhammad, the capital was, for a brilliant century, Damascus — a city close enough to the Mediterranean to remain part of the Hellenistic world. During this period Coptic and Greek were still spoken in Egypt and the administration was left in native hands. But when, in the eighth century, Baghdad became the caliphal center, Egypt was part of an empire increasingly dominated by Persians and Persian ideas.

For two centuries Egypt was the home province of an anticaliphate ruled by dynasts known, through their claimed descent from the Prophet's daughter Fatima, as Fatimids. These rulers, Tunisian warriors who conquered Egypt and a Middle Eastern empire including western Arabia and the Levant, were considered heretical by most of Islam. Their state collapsed in the twelfth century, and Egypt briefly enjoyed the rule of Saladin, a Kurd who proved the most exemplary Moslem ruler of all time. Linking Syria and Egypt in one state, he defeated the Crusaders.

Saladin's reign was a prelude to one of the most bizarre forms of human government, that of the Mamelukes, or white slaves. Islamic rulers had found it expedient to rely on Turkish-speaking hirelings to maintain civic order. These hirelings proved tougher and more reliable than dissident, free-born Arabs. The owned took over their owners — and from the middle of the thirteenth century until the Ottoman conquest in 1517, Egypt was ruled by white slaves who perpetuated their caste by importing recruits from the

The papyrus-shaped column (far left) that dominates the interior of the Moslem mosque of al-Maridani in Cairo is a memento of ancient Egypt. Similar pharaonic pillars adorn the nearby mihrab, *or sacred prayer-niche.*

slave markets of the Caucasus and Central Asia.

The Mameluke state was a feudal hierarchy in which speakers of Turkish did the fighting and ruling while the Arabic-speaking natives tilled the soil, traded, and prayed. Between the Arab conquest and the nineteenth century no native rose to high executive position. Only in religion — the obsession of Egyptians from earliest times — did the descendants of the pharaohs hold positions of influence. Al-Azhar, the great university-mosque founded by the Fatimids, played much the same role for Islam as the Temple of Re at Heliopolis had played in the past. The mosque's great pillared aisles, thronged by teachers and attentive students, became the powerhouse of Islamic orthodoxy. Since the rulers, whether Turkish or Circassian, were genuine Moslems, they respected an Egyptian judge for his knowledge of the sacred law; otherwise they looked on their dark-skinned subjects with disdain. They maintained this superior attitude even after their loss of sovereignty to the Ottomans.

Islamic rulers weakened or severed Egypt's links with the West. An exception were the Fatimids. Isolated inside Islam for their heretical opinions, they cultivated close relations with Sicily and southern Europe. The general separation worked to the disadvantage of Europe, whose early Middle Ages owed much of their darkness to this isolation from the East. For Egypt, the symbol of this separation was the decline of Alexandria. The once-glittering capital dwindled to a small fishing village, the Canopic mouth of the Nile dried up, and Rosetta — or in Arabic, Rashid — became the western port of the Nile delta.

In Alexandria's stead, a new Egyptian capital de-

veloped to the north of Babylon-in-Egypt, cut off from the salt sea but linked to the sand sea in which Arabs felt at home. It developed by stages. The first Islamic city grew up around the war tent from which Amr ruled his Arabian army. Al-Fustat — its name may derive from the Arabic word for tent — soon yielded to yet another city, a short distance to the north. The new capital was ruled by Ahmed ibn-Tulun, who made Egypt briefly independent from Baghdad even before the Fatimids. But the most important element in the future Cairo, the element that gave the city its name, was the Fatimid palace-city of Al-Kahira. Here the Fatimid caliphs reigned in semidivine mystery from behind a barricade of walls and slaves.

Islamic Egypt produced masterpieces of architecture; no other country in the Moslem world can show a similar development from the earliest to the most recent times. But these contributions — mosques, colleges, hospitals, and massive walls — were built at the command of non-Egyptians for a society of which Egypt was only a part. They belong more to a history of Islam than to the society that produced the pyramids; they form the back cloth to *The Arabian Nights* — and they deserve a volume to themselves.

Egypt retained a few links with the pharaonic past. Moslem rulers, like the pharaohs, used Nilometers, or wells into which the river flowed to be measured against a gauge. They also perpetuated the practice of throwing a doll, the "bride of the Nile," into the flooding river — a custom surviving from the time when a living virgin had been similarly thrown. Egyptians continued to bury their dead in "houses of eternity" modeled on the houses of everyday life. And

A thousand years after its foundation by the Fatimids, the mosque of al-Azhar remains Islam's foremost center for religious study. The graceful arcades that frame its inner courtyard offer an oasis for contemplation amid the bustle of modern Cairo.

until the twentieth century a major holiday of the year was the Coptic spring feast of *Shem el-Nesseem,* or "smelling of the breeze." But the monuments of the pharaonic past became as mysterious to Egyptians and Arabs as to Europeans. Medieval Cairo was probably the largest city on earth. From its multistory buildings, some crowned with roof gardens, visitors saw the still-intact pyramids on the Giza plateau. They went out to inspect them and wonder what their purpose could have been. Christians and Jews rubbed shoulders with Arab scholars and rulers. All were mystified. A popular explanation was that these giant buildings had been the granaries of Joseph, the patriarch who figured in the scriptures of all three faiths. A theory that appealed to Egypt's rulers was that the pyramids contained vast stores of gold.

In the hope of finding such treasure the caliph Mamun, on a visit from Baghdad, attacked the Great Pyramid. The scar made by his excavators is still visible above the entrance used today. The banging of Mamun's men dislodged a limestone block that for three thousand years had masked the corridor descending to the empty burial chamber beneath the ground. The sound made by this crashing megalith enabled the caliph's workmen to discover the system of corridors leading to the Grand Gallery — but they had come too late. Others had preceded them in the distant past, and the granite sarcophagus was probably as empty then as when the pyramids had last been sealed in the Twenty-sixth Dynasty.

Unable to read the hieroglyphs — which seemed but sinister representations of people and things — and unaware of the purpose of the pyramids, the rulers of Egypt used them and the considerable remains at Memphis as convenient sources of cut stone. When Saladin joined all the cities that clustered on the east bank — Babylon-in-Egypt, Amr's "City of the Tent," ibn-Tulun's town farther north, and Cairo itself — into one vast fortified *enceinte* based on the citadel, the need for such stone was particularly pressing.

At the end of the twelfth century, Saladin's son and heir had the presumptuous notion of demolishing the pyramids. He started on the smallest, the "red pyramid" of Mycerinus with its casing of Aswan granite. Drillers, stonecutters, and men coiled with ropes assembled near their intended victim. They found it almost as expensive to destroy as to build. Supervised by emirs, they and their horses stayed on the job eight months, a contemporary tells us. With all their efforts they were able to remove at most one or two stones each day, and this at the cost of tiring themselves utterly. Some were charged to move the stones forward with wedges and levers; others tugged at them from below with cords and cables. When at last one of the stones fell, it made a tremendous noise that reverberated far off, shaking the very earth and making the hills tremble. In its fall the stone would bury itself in the sand, thus requiring extraordinary efforts to free it. By means of wedges the stones were split into several pieces; each single piece required a cart to carry it to the foot of the escarpment, where it was left. The contemporary account concludes that after great expense of time and money "so far from accomplishing what they had set out to do, they had merely spoiled the pyramid and shown themselves incapable."

Medieval accounts of the pyramids show extremes

of accuracy and absurdity. An Iraqi physician, Abdul Latif al-Baghdadi, focused a shrewd mind on the monuments. (Abdul Latif was the only medieval doctor to add to the legacy of the Greek physician Galen. He did so thanks to an Egyptian famine, which enabled him to study dead bodies, a thing until then taboo. Among other things, Abdul Latif found Galen's statement that the lower jawbone consisted of two separate bones joined at the chin to be untrue. Even more remarkable in an age that worshiped established authority, Abdul Latif published his contradictory findings.)

The pyramid shape impressed Abdul Latif as eminently suitable for gigantic monuments. "The center of gravity is the center of the building itself. Since it presses on itself, since itself supports the whole pressure of this mass, all its parts bear respectively one upon the other, and it does not press on any external point." Abdul Latif entered the Great Pyramid through the hole made by the caliph. But after climbing two-thirds of the way to the tomb chamber he turned back, assailed by the stench of bat dung.

Unlike Herodotus, Abdul Latif noticed the Sphinx:

A little more than a bowshot from these pyramids is a colossal figure of a head and neck projecting from the earth. The name of this is Abu'l-Hol and the body to which the head belongs is said to be buried under the earth. If the dimensions of the head are a clue to those of the body, it must be more than seventy cubits long. On the face is a reddish tint, and a red varnish as bright as if freshly put on. The face is remarkably beautiful; the mouth in particular has a charming expression; it seems to be smiling gently.

Another traveler of the same period, this one from Granada in Moorish Spain, illustrates how the eye can see what the mind tells it to. Ibn-Jubayr compared the pyramids to "huge pavilions rearing into the skies." Even odder was his description of the Sphinx: "a strange figure of stone rising up like a minaret in the form of a man of fearsome aspect. Its face is toward the pyramids." The Sphinx, in fact, faces away from the pyramids and toward the rising sun. To account at all for the minaret comparison, we must remember that sands had again covered the leonine body and that minarets had not yet become the slender candles of Turkish times. But in seeing the Sphinx as fearsome, ibn-Jubayr was typical of a people whose greatest skill was in words and on whom words had a mesmeric effect. Misled by its Arab nickname, Abu'l-Hol, or Father of Terror, he had attributed to the Sphinx all the fearsomeness that the name implied.

Even this level of interest in the Egyptian past declined after the sixteenth century. In the late Middle Ages the Mameluke state ruled Palestine and Syria as well as Egypt; it thus controlled the major route to the East, source of the spices so coveted in the dull kitchens of Europe. This made Egypt rich and desirable. But once the Portuguese had discovered the sea route around Africa, Egypt declined in importance. The Ottomans conquered this diminished Egypt in 1517 and then left it to the tender care of the Mamelukes, who collected taxes on their behalf. By the end of the eighteenth century the population had shrunk from the seven million of classical times to perhaps two million; the Fayum oasis, once the greatest area of Greek influence and agriculture, had fallen into dere-

liction thanks to Bedouin incursions; and the Mamelukes had used the Sphinx for target practice — which accounts for much of the damage to that august face.

It was ill-omened sacrilege. For within range of the pyramids and Sphinx was fought the 1798 battle that at last weakened Mameluke power. The victor was the young Corsican general Napoleon Bonaparte, who had just disembarked a considerable army near Alexandria. His strategic aim was to sever Britain's land connections with India. But a secondary purpose, more in tune with "The Marseillaise," had inspired Napoleon to bring with him a brigade of scholars as well as fonts for printing Arabic and Greek.

Napoleon's strategic purpose was to be thwarted by his inability to control the Mediterranean. This was made painfully evident when the British admiral Nelson destroyed the French fleet anchored in the bay of Aboukir; the French army was thus marooned in a country that it controlled but would ultimately have to leave. After a stay as short as Alexander the Great's, Napoleon slipped back to Paris and his military obsessions.

For Egypt and the world, Napoleon's invasion had lasting consequences. The presence of a French army in Cairo initiated a double process whereby Egypt rediscovered the West and, with gathering momentum, the outside world rediscovered Egypt. Egypt's emergence as a modern state and the modern science of Egyptology both have their beginnings in the French invasion.

The Egyptians, despite long isolation and oppression, retained the talents that had distinguished their forebears. While resisting the French in their role as foreign intruders, they were impressed by the evidence of French cultural and scientific progress displayed in Napoleon's Institut d'Egypte in Cairo and by such innovations as libraries, where ordinary French soldiers read printed books, and cafes, where both sexes mixed in public. Throughout the nineteenth century increasing waves of French influence were to roll over Egyptian society, creating what purists might call a hybrid civilization, but which to the people concerned represented an attempt to retain their own soul while importing those aspects of modernity — from medical service to street lighting, from lighthouses to railways — that could make life more congenial. It was the same process whereby, in the distant past, the pharaohs had introduced the horse-drawn chariot or the iron sword.

The man who applied the lessons taught by the French came, by a strange coincidence, from the very area that had produced Alexander and the Ptolemies. Muhammad Ali, the rebuilder of Alexandria and the founder of modern Egypt, was born in Macedonia. As a loyal subject of the Ottoman sultan, who was the nominal sovereign of Egypt, he had landed in Egypt during the French occupation to help his fellow Moslems, the Mamelukes, against the infidels. Muhammad Ali did nothing effective on this score — but after the French army had been evacuated he progressively made himself the country's all-but-independent ruler. The destruction of the Mamelukes begun by Napoleon was completed by a ruthless massacre that violated the Eastern canons of hospitality: the Mamelukes were invited to drink coffee in the citadel, and then slaughtered as they defiled through a narrow place on horseback.

Firmly in power, Muhammad Ali dragooned Egypt into becoming a westernizing kingdom, and throughout the nineteenth century his descendants carried on the process. They imported southern Europeans as the Ptolemies had done long before. But these were not poets or pure scientists; they were often shrewd businessmen motivated by the opportunity to make money. Such strategists of the age of steel helped Muhammad Ali's Egypt to build one of the world's earliest railway networks, to develop cotton into a major crop, to link Cairo with Alexandria by means of a canal, and to turn the latter city into a great new gateway to the West. Just as Alexandria's dereliction had symbolized Egypt's isolation from the West, so its revival symbolized Egypt's return to contact with Europe.

The most fateful decision of Muhammad Ali's dynasty was to allow the construction of the Suez Canal. That sea-to-sea waterway — begun under Said Pasha, who gave his name to one port, and completed under Khedive Ismail, who gave his name to another — put Egypt once again at the nodal point of world communications. Imperial Britain had opposed the digging of the canal; her statesmen feared that it might enable enemies to approach the Indian Empire. Once it was built, however, the British government recognized the canal's importance, and taking advantage of Ismail's indebtedness, it secured a major holding in the Suez Canal Company. Soon thereafter Britain used the pretext of a nationalistic revolution to turn the country into a veiled protectorate. The effect on Egyptian public opinion was predictable: to admiration for European techniques and culture was added resentment of the Europeans' will-to-power and racial arrogance.

The French view of the battle of the Nile, as reflected in the nineteenth-century decorative plate at left, portrays the future emperor as an all-conquering hero. England's perspective was far less flattering: in 1815, the year of Napoleon's defeat at Waterloo, illustrator George Cruikshank drew the satiric cartoon below showing Napoleon in precipitate retreat from the land of the pyramids and Sphinx.

All knowledge of the meaning of Egyptian hieroglyphics — such as those inscribed on a column (left) from a Sixth Dynasty tomb at Sakkara — had been lost for centuries when, in 1799, a French officer found an irregularly shaped black basalt tablet near the port of Rosetta. The deciphering of the Rosetta Stone (right) by Jean François Champollion made possible the rediscovery of the incomparable culture of ancient Egypt.

Nineteenth-century Europeans, propelled by an impetus as confident as railway pistons, hardly took seriously the stirrings of modern Egypt. What they did take seriously, in a spiritual vacation from their age of steel, was ancient Egypt. It appealed to them as it had done long before to the rationalistic Greeks. Egyptian motifs influenced the Empire furniture of France; the country with its balmy winter climate became one of the first places to be developed by the new industry of tourism, democratic successor to the aristocratic Grand Tour.

An archaeological accident and the use made of it by a young Frenchman played a vital role in the rediscovery of ancient Egypt. During the Napoleonic occupation the country's chief port was still Rosetta. Outside a fortress some miles from the port a French officer unearthed, in 1799, a basalt block large enough to require a sturdy wheelbarrow, its polished side inscribed with letters. When the French army left Egypt in 1801, it surrendered the Rosetta Stone to the British, who later gave it a place of honor in the British Museum. Under hands that knew how to work the lock, the Rosetta Stone was to prove a door to the long-mute world of Egyptian writing.

An untutored eye could see that the stone bore three distinct scripts. One was in legible Greek; another was in the hieroglyphics already familiar from temple walls; the third was less immediately recognizable. The Greek text was almost intact, and in an age when Greek was understood by schoolboys it was easily deciphered. The inscription recorded that the priests of Egypt, assembled at Memphis in 196 B.C., had issued a decree in honor of Ptolemy V. It seemed likely that

the two other scripts repeated the same message. It also seemed likely that the third script was what Herodotus had described as the demotic version of the hieroglyphic writing.

The first significant step in deciphering the hieroglyphics was helped by the ropelike rings, or cartouches, that surrounded certain groups of hieroglyphs. Eighteenth-century visitors to Egypt correctly suggested that these "royal rings" contained the names of rulers. British Quaker Thomas Young (1773–1829) is known to history as the author of the undulatory theory of light and first describer of the optical condition known as astigmatism. But this brilliant physician was also a gifted linguist who had mastered seven languages, including Hebrew, Arabic, and Persian, by the time he was fourteen. In 1818 he correctly identified several of the names in the Rosetta Stone's cartouches by comparing them with the proper names in the Greek text.

To Young, Egyptology was never more than a sideline. In sharp contrast, Young's youthful French contemporary Jean François Champollion (1790–1832) felt that he had been called by destiny to unpuzzle the ancient Egyptian script and language. He had prepared himself for this task by making a thorough study of Coptic, the last form of the pharaonic tongue. Champollion had been able to do this thanks to manuscripts brought back from Egypt by seventeenth-century travelers and thanks to later spadework on the language by Jesuit scholars. Using copies of the Rosetta Stone cartouches — combined with others carved on an obelisk and plinth in the possession of an English country gentleman and reproduced by lithograph —

The awesome ruin of the temple of Amen-Re at Karnak, seen in the photograph at right, evokes the splendor of ancient Egypt. No less impressive are the two mutilated statues below, dubbed the Colossi of Memnon by the Greeks in honor of their mythical hero. In fact, these seventy-foot-high red sandstone figures are likenesses of the pharaoh Amenhotep III. The funerary temple they once guarded has long since vanished, and today the "colossi" stand in isolation on the plains of west-bank Thebes.

Champollion quickly deciphered every one of the Greco-Roman names, including Ptolemaeus and Cleopatra. He broke into the silent world of pharaonic writing proper when he identified the name of Ramesses on a temple inscription by recognizing that the sun-symbol stood for the word *re*, the Coptic word for sun. By 1824, when he published his *Summary of the Hieroglyphic System,* he could decipher almost all the inscriptions he discovered on frequent visits to Muhammad Ali's Egypt.

As late as the eighteenth century many scholars, even those who had done masterly work on Coptic, had considered hieroglyphics as mere symbols. Champollion revealed that they formed a complete if complex form of writing capable of expressing the full range of meaning, in a language partly Semitic and partly African. The complexity was due to the fact that a hieroglyph could play one of several distinctive roles. It could stand, like ⊙ , for an idea — in this case the sun — and also for a syllable — in this case *re*. It could also stand for an individual consonant in what amounted to a pharaonic alphabet. (Later discoveries in Sinai strongly suggested that the Phoenician script, parent of all Western alphabets, had been derived from such hieroglyphs.) In addition, it could stand as a determinative, a symbol making it clear whether the preceding hieroglyphs represented a god, a man, a mammal, a building, a river — or a whole range of other generic types.

Champollion's short life laid the basis for the philological approach to Egyptology. King-lists on temple walls; letters from merchants, diplomats, and schoolboys; reports of battles or trials; stories and funerary

texts — all would illuminate what it had been like to live in ancient Egypt. But while language can lead us into men's thoughts, it is often the tool of propagandists and special pleaders; it can also conceal or misrepresent. Such important nonpersons as Hashepsowe or Akhenaten would owe their rediscovery not to the pen of the philologist but to the spade of the digger.

The digging side of Egyptology was initiated by more questionable champions of the ancient civilization than Champollion. Napoleon's Egyptian adventure — which he later described as "the most beautiful in my life, because it was the most ideal" — inspired an interest in Egypt that soon developed into a voracious hunger for Egyptian relics. The possession of a national collection of statues, mummies, or papyri became almost as much a sign of nationhood as a colonial empire. Adventurers on the spot in Egypt, often working with European consuls, helped start the collections that now embellish museums in Paris, Leyden, Berlin, and London. When, at the opening of the Suez Canal in 1869, the Austrian emperor complained that Vienna lacked its quota, Khedive Ismail showed his guest to a large room stacked with treasures — and in the hospitable manner of the East, invited the emperor to take his pick.

The rape of Egypt was as thorough as the rape of Mexico by the conquistadores, if less cruel. European collectors had willing allies in the fellahin, who suddenly found that their hovels crouched over gold mines. Of such robber-archaeologists the most destructive was the Frenchman Emile Amélineau, who did not shrink from smashing part of a cache of pots to maintain the market price of the survivors. The most

energetic was Giovanni Belzoni, a gigantic Italian with as varied talents as Thomas Young. After abandoning the cloister for which he was intended, Belzoni studied to be a hydraulic engineer — only to be forced by poverty to earn his living as a circus strongman. In Egypt, Belzoni secured the patronage of British traveler, antiquarian, and consul-general Henry Salt. Belzoni failed to sell Muhammad Ali a scheme for raising the waters of the Nile, but he did find in the exploitation of pharaonic antiquities a means of raising funds for himself.

Belzoni's energy in a hot and still risky climate was prodigious: he cleared the sand from the gigantic rock-temple of Ramesses II at Abu Simbel, deep inside Nubia; he shipped the colossal bust of the same megalomaniac pharaoh from Luxor to the British Museum; he was the first man in modern times to penetrate the long despoiled burial chamber of Chephren in the second pyramid. In addition he swept through the Valley of the Kings like a vacuum cleaner, discovered the beautifully painted tomb of Seti I, and then announced that the valley was empty. Moreover, the Italian strongman had a natural talent for publicity. In an "Egyptian Hall" in Piccadilly, he enthralled all London with facsimiles of the wall paintings from Seti's tomb. This Byron of Egyptology died a year before the poet; in 1823, on an expedition to West Africa — a prelude to the European annexation of that vast area — he succumbed to dysentery.

Even the stalwart pyramids were not safe from this first, clumsy generation of explorers. Two Englishmen — Colonel Howard Vyse and John Shea Perring — were so determined to bare the secrets of the pyramids

that they used a tool unknown to previous entrants. Vexed with mortar that proved to be nearly as hard as the stone itself, and aware of how long it would take Arab workmen to break it down, Colonel Vyse used gunpowder "with great effect." By these violent methods, Vyse and Perring penetrated to the chambers above the burial chamber of Cheops.

In the third pyramid, which had long since been robbed, the pair discovered the magnificent sarcophagus of Mycerinus. For patriotic Englishmen of this period, the world was centered on London. A generation earlier the seventh Lord Elgin had shipped the Parthenon friezes to the British Museum; Vyse and Perring crated this Egyptian relic for delivery to the same address. Both decisions were archaeologically harmful. The climate of Dickensian London did more damage to the Elgin Marbles in a hundred years than the air of Attica had done in over two thousand. And the sarcophagus of Mycerinus fared worse: it was shipwrecked on its journey north and now lies at the bottom of the sea.

The approach to the pyramids was not only greedy and brutal, it was also superstitious. There was, in the century of Darwin and Edison, an extraordinary reversal to the ancient view of Egypt as a land of mystery. A school of what was known as pyramidologists proliferated in the shadow of a considerable oak tree: Charles Piazzi Smyth. Piazzi Smyth, whose life spanned the nineteenth century, was made astronomer royal of Scotland at the early age of twenty-six after describing both Halley's comet and the great comet of 1843. A kink in Piazzi Smyth's otherwise straight life was his "discovery" of the Pyramid Inch, a measurement

which he defined as being 1.001 of a British inch and which, applied to the innards of the Great Pyramid, foretold the whole sweep of human history from the deluge to the rise of the British Empire. One twist in the staircase would mark the Crucifixion, another the battle of Waterloo, a third the repeal of the Corn Laws. Piazzi Smyth had no patience with pharaonic culture. To him, the builders of the pyramids belonged to a great Adamic race — white, of course — that spoke across the centuries to that pyramid of states, the British Empire.

The pyramidologists outlasted the railway age and were active well into the century of Rutherford and Marconi. Most of them were Anglo-Saxons; a significant number were retired sailors or generals; not one was a serious scientist of the order of Piazzi Smyth. Their basic assumption seems to have sprung from emotional logic: the pyramids were the greatest wonders of the ancient world; ancient Egyptians had been a superstitious, dark-skinned people unlike the British; the British Empire, the greatest state in history, was ruled by white people professing a monotheistic creed; therefore the pyramids must have been built by some white protoimperial race. Piazzi Smyth indeed argued that the pyramids were not built by Egyptians at all, but by the "Sethic" forebears of the Hebrews.

By an amusing irony, pyramidology led to the exact study of the pyramids rather as astrology had led to astronomy. Flinders Petrie, the son of one of Piazzi Smyth's disciples, went to Egypt as a young man to confirm the master's measurements. Petrie soon discovered that Piazzi Smyth's basic measurements were

In spite of his highly unorthodox methods, Italian archaeologist Giovanni Belzoni — seen at far left as an Oriental potentate — made a significant contribution to Egyptology. The whimsical engravings of workmen removing the rubble from a pyramid (left) and carting off a colossal head of Ramesses II (right) are from Belzoni's own record of his highly successful expedition to Egypt.

all wrong, and that one of the elder man's followers, a Mr. Glover, had even tried to file down a projecting boss of stone in the anteroom to the King's Chamber to make it equal the Pyramid Inch. Petrie's *The Pyramids and Temples of Gizeh*, published when he was only thirty, represents the first application of spade and ruler in a very long and useful life. At Abydos in Upper Egypt, the chief center of the Osiris cult, Petrie uncovered the tombs of the early dynastic kings, first stage in the architectural process that culminated in the pyramids. At Tell el-Amarna his spade again uncovered the lost world of Akhenaten's utopia.

Petrie symbolized a changed attitude toward the past. Knowledge, not salable objets d'art, became the chief target of research. Control over sites rich in antiquities, control over the fellahin who dug them up, control over the methods of recording and preserving finds, steadily pushed back the frontiers of knowledge about ancient Egypt. Thanks to the controlled archaeology of men like Petrie, we now know more of the appearance and lives of pharaonic Egyptians than we do of Saxon Englishmen.

Control over would-be robbers was established with difficulty; control over archaeological method was established through trial and error. Two spectacular finds — one illuminating the personages of some of the greatest pharaohs, the other illuminating the lives of ordinary people — exemplify the way in which control and chance can work together.

Ever since the time of Belzoni the Upper Egyptian town of Luxor, standing as it does near the ruins of Thebes, had been the center of a vast trade in ancient objects. The prime source for these was the west-

bank village of Gurna, built on the flanks of the bare Theban hills. The Gurna family of Ahmed Abdul Rasoul, backed by their wealthy European contacts, was more than a match for the complex Ottoman law that theoretically prohibited the export of national treasures. But after the opening of the Suez Canal, a new mood of national responsibility developed, symbolized by the appointment of Sir Gaston Maspero as keeper of Cairo Museum. A sense of caution now dominated the Gurna people. Then one night in 1871, while prowling the barren hills for treasure, Abdul Rasoul stumbled upon a secret three thousand years old: the coffins of thirty-six pharaohs reburied in a lonely shaft by Twenty-first Dynasty priests.

For ten years the Gurna family acted with secretive prudence, milking their astonishing find of only such small, easily sold objects as would embellish a London study or a Paris drawing room: scarabs, seals, canopic jars, statuettes of Osiris, and papyrus fragments were all eagerly sought by wintering Europeans. By 1881 — a year in which the clash between Egyptian nationalism and the British Empire was coming to a head — reports of the persistent sale of objects relating to the Twenty-first Dynasty focused official curiosity on the hills behind Gurna.

After interrogation — a euphemism for the Ottoman practice of whipping a suspect's bare soles — Abdul Rasoul coughed out his secret. In July 1881 the assistant keeper of Cairo Museum was taken up the scorching cliff face and lowered down the shaft to confront a deposit that scorched his eyes. Here, now that hieroglyphs were as intelligible as Greek, were legible dockets attached to the mummies of some formidable

figures in Egyptian history: Tuthmosis III, Seti I, and Ramesses II among them. The mummies were not in their original wrappings or coffins but had evidently been hastily reinterred; some had been through the process of reburial as many as three times.

Two hundred Upper Egyptians were needed to carry the mummies in their heavy coffins across rocks and plain to the Nile. Loaded onto a steamer they were shipped north to the new Cairo Museum. As the boat with its weird freight passed, the fellahin on both banks performed the funeral rites of modern Egypt, the men shooting off their guns, the women wailing.

The mummies, treated with less respect by officials, are proof of the abject failure of burial shafts to protect a gold-wrapped god from greedy mortals. A document survives detailing the circumstances in which some Twentieth Dynasty tomb-robbers were tried. One robber attests:

> We opened their sarcophagi and the coffins in which they lay and found the august mummy of this King equipped with a falchion; many amulets and golden ornaments were upon his neck and his golden headpiece was upon him. The august mummy of this King was entirely bedecked with gold, and his coffins were adorned with gold and silver inside and out and inlaid with all manner of precious stone. We amassed the gold we found on the noble mummy of this god. . . .

A god — yet in pursuit of gold the robbers had burned his coffin and that of his queen before fleeing.

The Gurna coffins were not the only cache hidden by pious priests. In 1893 the tomb of Amenhotep II

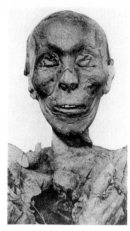
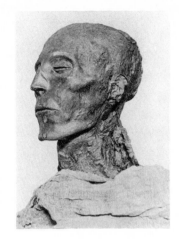

was opened by a French architect and found to contain another thirteen: these included the mummies of Tuthmosis IV, who cleared the Sphinx of sand, and Amenhotep III, Akhenaten's father.

These mummies, lying boxed in Cairo Museum, enable us to see that the mortician's art could bequeath only caricatures of men. Tuthmosis II, the divine husband of Hashepsowe, has a wasted, concentration camp look; a scream of anguish against time hurls mutely through his open mouth. Tuthmosis III, the king, articulate conqueror, has a little noseless head, black with years, and his intact teeth seem to chuckle at a secret joke. His mummy is wrapped in what looks like inexpensive cheesecloth. Tuthmosis IV, who so loved hunting, has his head wrenched permanently back as though forever riding a spectral carriage — his lips just open, his hair matted as though from a swim through mud; his flesh wooden. The pharaohs of the following dynasty, the Nineteenth, are evidently of a different mold. Seti I has a head like a piece of sculpture, the jaw still strong, the nose peremptory and hooked. Merneptah, long fancied as the pharaoh of the Exodus, looks the most regal: a pottery pharaoh with the powerful Ramesside nose and what look like painted eyebrows.

The two rulers who were never found, Hashepsowe and Akhenaten, may have had the best of the bargain. To be gazed on by any tourist who can afford the entrance fee of 25 piastres (or a little more than 50 cents) is not what any self-respecting pharaoh would have wished for his *ka*.

If the cache of mummies brings us eerily close to the great ones of the past, another discovery, made within a short distance of where the royal corpses were found, gives us an astonishing glimpse of the ordinary people who were, until 1920, absentees from our vision of the pharaonic world. The discoverer was an American, H. E. Winlock, making a routine examination of the long-looted tomb of Meket-Re, a chancellor and steward of the royal palace who lived around 2000 B.C.:

> At court his influence must have been considerable, for he chose the choicest spot in the necropolis of his day, directly overlooking the place where his sovereign's own mortuary temple was being built. The site is weirdly impressive. The great buttressed cliffs of tawny limestone practically enclose a deep circus a quarter of a mile in diameter. . . . High above, around the rim of the circus where the cliffs start vertically upward, are the black mouths of the tombs of the courtiers. Meket-Re had chosen the side of a mountain spur, grading the slope until he had an avenue 25 yards wide and 80 yards long, which climbed the hill at an angle of 20° — an angle steep enough to get the average person in quite a puffy state by the time he had toiled up to the top.

After eight profitless weeks of work in the nearby valley, Winlock and his men were planning to give the emptied tomb one further week. Then on Wednesday, March 17, 1920, toward sunset, an Egyptian worker noticed chips of stone trickling from his hoe into a crevice. Winlock was told the exciting news. The team approached the crack in the dark, and one by one, lying flat on the ground, each man shone a flashlight through it, revealing "one of the most startling sights it is ever a digger's luck to see. . . ."

The secret underground burial chambers in the Valley of the Kings, designed to house royal bodies for all eternity, proved easy prey for determined tomb thieves. Among the comparatively few mummies that escaped defilement are the three wizened souls at left — the pharaohs Merneptah, Tuthmosis II, and Seti I. The mummy of the court official Meket-Re disappeared thousands of years ago; yet, in anticipation of an afterlife that would encompass the best features of earthly existence, his tomb was equipped with brightly painted wooden models (right) of a weaving shop (top), a granary (center), and a slaughterhouse (bottom).

The party had come upon a little secret room that had escaped the attention of four millennia of robbers. That room did not contain funerary objects; on the contrary, it contained the most vivid portrayals of everyday life in ancient Egypt ever to be uncovered: Eleventh Dynasty representations that bring ordinary men and women alive in the context of their daily occupations. Twenty-four models — now shared by the Cairo Museum and the Metropolitan Museum in New York — evoke the life of a landed proprietor during the period of Egyptian history — the Middle Kingdom — that exemplified the *maat,* or order, which the pharaonic world extolled.

A chancellor such as Meket-Re would have used the Nile as frequently as a modern administrator uses an airplane or car, and consequently four of the models are ships, each about four feet long. Sailing south, against the current, these small figures hoist a great square sail, the sailors hauling on the halyards. Going north, with the current, they lower the mast and stow the sail on deck, the crew steering the boat with oars and a great stern paddle. As for Meket-Re, he sniffs a lotus bud in his chair while beside him a blind harpist accompanies a singer. In reality, such ships would have been thirty or forty feet long — too small, as Winlock points out, for cooking on board to be convenient. So a kitchen boat follows, ready to come alongside at mealtimes. On board, women grind flour and men bake; joints of meat hang in the cabins and jars of beer and wine are stored in racks.

Meket-Re wished to be buried with these evocative models of all that he did and owned, and as a result his world survives. But though he is central, he does

not overpower. Our interest focuses as much on his environment as on his person. There are, for example, two unique models of pleasure gardens. In one, a high wall ensures privacy and a pillared veranda looks out on an oblong pool of copper surrounded by seven sycamores. "The trees, made of wood, have each little leaf carved and pegged in place," H. E. Winlock notes in his book *Excavations at Deir el-Bahri*. "The fruit is not growing from the twigs, but from the main stems and branches, so that there shall be no doubt but that the sycamore fig is intended."

There are scenes of cattle being fattened and slaughtered, of baking and brewing, of spinning and weaving, of the squaring and sawing of timber. But the model that most evokes the order of Egyptian life is a superb tableau of an event important on every Egyptian estate: the counting of the cattle. The landlord sits in the shade of a four-pillared porch in front of his house. Nineteen longhorned beasts — some with big black patches on white, some yellow-patched, some mottled, one red — suggest his herds. Four scribes squat beside the landlord for the count while a delinquent is brought before them under the upheld rod of another servant. The model evokes a hierarchical society, but not one of lowering domination. All are engaged in work that they know to be important. All the men — the landlord, his heir, the scribes, the delinquent and the obedient servant, the drovers — are the same size; all wear identical kilt-like garments that leave the upper torso bare. All work together in agrarian sanity, the basis of Egyptian wealth throughout the ages and the very subsoil from which Osiris sprang.

Meket-Re's miniature treasures included a procession
of figures bearing ritual offerings (left below) and a
tableau of the master presiding over an inspection of
his cattle (below). The wooden model at left, from a
Twelfth Dynasty tomb, shows household servants
baking bread, brewing beer, and skinning an ox.

VIII

The Past Recaptured

By the end of World War I, a century had elapsed since Champollion first deciphered the hieroglyphic system and Belzoni brought back the first statues and paintings to astonish London. Although a morning haze still enveloped the early dynasties and smoke still obscured the intermediate hollows, the mist had cleared from the major heights on the pharaonic landscape. The Old World's most spectacular civilization was no longer a labyrinth where Herodotus and his informants were the only guides, where every mystagogue could find his patron. The purposes of the pyramids were understood; the tools of those who had built them, the rigging of the ships that had brought the granite from Aswan, the utensils from which the workmen ate and drank — all were precisely known. If the dates of the earliest pharaohs were still in doubt, the agrarian society they ruled — the world in which male Egyptians plowed, worshiped, or fought; the world in which their women wove flax, instructed children, or danced — was now familiar. Enough statues had been dredged from the sand, enough tomb paintings copied or photographed, to make of the people who molded this civilization our neighbors in time.

Most of those surviving statues or objects were either too cumbrous to carry or untempting to thieves. The pyramids themselves had been saved from caliphs and colonels by their sheer mass, and remoteness as well as size had protected the two colossal temples at Abu Simbel. The diorite statue of Chephren, his head enfolded by the wings of Horus, was unearthed with eight others — all broken — in a well near his valley temple; statues of Queen Hashepsowe and Akhenaten were reassembled from mutilated fragments; and the mummies of the other pharaohs were found to be little more than desiccated kernels, their golden husks having long since been peeled away.

If a tomb's mere sweepings could be so rich, its contents when full would have been a treasure indeed. The great Egyptologists of the nineteenth century must have lamented — in French or English, German or Italian — that no burial chamber at Memphis or Thebes had ever been found intact. Having lamented, they may have prayed for the good fortune of coming upon one inviolate pharaoh or his queen.

Egypt is a place for the offering and granting of prayers, and the 1920's were marked by two miracles of astonishing amplitude. The first and more spectacular — the discovery of an Eighteenth Dynasty pharaoh asleep in his golden coffin — was the triumph of an Englishman, Howard Carter; the historically more important — the recovery of the funerary treasure of Hetep-Heres, the first queen of the Fourth Dynasty — was the achievement of an American archaeologist, George Andrew Reisner.

Howard Carter had inherited a talent for drawing from his father, an artist who had specialized in painting the household pets of the Victorian British. While still in his teens, Carter put his talent to work in Egypt, where he copied the tomb reliefs, at Tel el-Amarna and elsewhere, discovered by diggers such as Flinders Petrie. By 1907 he had acquired a considerable knowledge of Egyptology but lacked the financial means for independent work. Sir Gaston Maspero, keeper of the Cairo Museum, therefore introduced him to the fifth Earl of Carnarvon, a rich amateur in need of expert help. Carnarvon, one of the world's

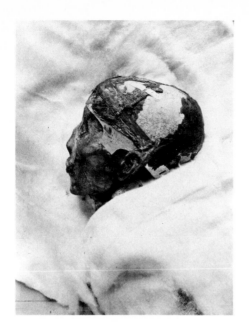

This photograph of the head of Tutankhamen was taken at the time the mummy was removed from the multiple coffins and shrines in which it had reposed for more than three thousand years.

first victims of an automobile accident, had been severely injured while on holiday in Germany in a collision involving his vehicle and two bullock carts. Before his accident, the earl had been an outdoor sports enthusiast; now he diverted his powerful energies into aesthetic channels. He amassed an important collection. "My chief aim," he later said of it, "was then, and is now, not merely to buy because a thing is rare, but rather to consider the beauty of an object [more] than its pure historic value."

Carnarvon's interest in excavation was aroused when, after his accident, he spent a winter convalescing in Luxor. The influence of a senior British official in the Egyptian government secured this aristocratic beginner a permit to spend the winter of 1906 digging at Thebes, where Carnarvon uncovered one large mummified cat. Maspero saw the desirability of channeling this wealth and enthusiasm in more fruitful directions. His suggestion that Carnarvon should employ Carter as his assistant led to a partnership that, after fifteen years, achieved a triumphant climax. The triumph was well earned.

Although the two men published a sumptuous volume entitled *Five Years' Exploration at Thebes* in 1912, they had made only routine discoveries up to that point. They were then separated by World War I, Carnarvon and his wife turning their country house into a hospital for wounded officers, Carter remaining in Egypt. The peace of 1919 found Egypt in nationalist revolt against the British and Carnarvon in diminishing health. With some misgivings, for he was the kind of rich man who wants a substantial return for his outlay, the earl had continued to subsidize Carter.

And Carter in turn had persisted through six frustrating seasons, fired by an inner certainty that objects found in the valley by an earlier digger, Theodore Davis, proved that somewhere nearby lay Tutankhamen, the transitional boy-king who had led Egypt back from Akhenaten's heresy to the orthodoxy of Amen-Re.

"We had worked for months at a stretch," Carter wrote of his *annus mirabilis*, "and found nothing, and only an excavator knows how desperately depressing that can be; we had almost made up our minds that we were beaten, and were preparing to leave The Valley and try our luck elsewhere; and then — hardly had we set hoe to ground in our last despairing effort than we made a discovery that far exceeded our wildest dreams."

Near the long-explored tomb of Ramesses VI in the middle of the valley, a group of roughly built workmen's huts that had been erected in ancient times had lingered on as ruins. As part of his last, desperate throw, Carter told his workmen to clear these away. When he arrived at the site on the morning of November 4, 1922, he immediately noticed the excitement on his workmen's faces. Under the very first hut a stone step had been uncovered. Now that Carter had come, hoes bit swiftly into the dust. The step was only the first of a flight of sixteen leading down to a walled-up door.

Carter now needed the patience of a saint. Suppressing his desire to forge ahead, he cabled Carnarvon: "At last we have made a wonderful discovery in Valley; a magnificent tomb with seal intact; re-covered same for your arrival; congratulations."

119

Dogged determination and skillful searching in the Valley of the Kings reaped the most remarkable archaeological find in history. Amid long-abandoned workers' huts and the rubble of earlier digs, Englishman Howard Carter uncovered the entrance to the tomb of Tutankhamen, situated behind the low retaining wall (right foreground) in the photograph below. Within the underground sepulcher, Carter found an unusual painted and stuccoed wooden statue (right) of the boy-king. Scholars speculate that the figure may have been intended as a "dressmaker's dummy" since only the torso and head were completed.

Traveling by ship and train, Carnarvon and his daughter, Lady Evelyn Herbert, reached Egypt on November 20 and Luxor three days later. On the following day Carter and his assistant, in the presence of Carnarvon, removed the rubble with which they had masked the door. On examining the door more thoroughly, they found that the seal impressions on the lower section were much clearer than those above, and on several the name of Tutankhamen was easily legible. "This added enormously," Carter wrote later, "to the interest of the discovery. If we had found, as seemed almost certain, the tomb of that shadowy monarch, whose tenure of the throne coincided with one of the most interesting periods of Egyptian history, we should indeed have reason to congratulate ourselves." But closer examination aroused misgivings. It was clear that in pharaonic times the doorway had been breached and resealed on two occasions.

Examination of the rubbish at the bottom of the stairs increased the archaeologists' sense of unease. Broken pottery, scarabs, the useless detritus of pharaohs as separate in time as Tuthmosis III and Akhenaten, made it seem possible that the tomb had been emptied, then used to store a cache of miscellaneous objects. Two anxious days were spent removing the doorway and clearing the rubble-filled descending corridor that led, after some thirty feet, to a second sealed doorway almost identical to the first. November 26 was the most wonderful day Carter had ever lived through, and certainly one whose like he could never hope to see again. In the late afternoon it was decided to pierce this second door. Those present were now almost certain that they would find only a store, not

an intact tomb. Carter's stirring account deserves to be quoted in full:

The decisive moment had arrived. With trembling hands I made a tiny breach in the upper left hand corner. Darkness and black space, as far as an iron testing-rod could reach, showed that whatever lay beyond was empty, and not filled like the passage we had just cleared. Candle tests were applied as a precaution against possible foul gases, and then, widening the hole a little, I inserted the candle and peered in, Lord Carnarvon, Lady Evelyn and Callender standing anxiously beside me to hear the verdict. At first I could see nothing, the hot air escaping from the chamber causing the candle flame to flicker, but presently, as my eyes grew accustomed to the light, details of the room within emerged slowly from the mist, strange animals, statues, and gold — everywhere the glint of gold. For the moment — an eternity it must have seemed to the others standing by — I was struck dumb with amazement, and when Lord Carnarvon, unable to stand the suspense any longer, inquired anxiously, "Can you see anything?" it was all I could do to get out the words, "Yes, wonderful things." Then widening the hole a little further, so that we could both see, we inserted an electric torch.

What Carter found beyond the wall was not fully revealed to an impatient world for another eleven years, for he was a meticulous scientist, not a showman. His careful approach is indicated by the publication dates of the three volumes in which he describes *The Tomb of Tut.Ankh.Amen.* The first volume, which appeared in 1923, described the antechamber. The

Each step in the painstaking process of investigating Tutankhamen's tomb was recorded by photographer Harry Burton. At right is a view of the disordered jumble of priceless objects and worthless debris that littered much of the interior. At far right, Carter — under the watchful gaze of his patron, Lord Carnarvon — prepares to wrap for transport one of the life-size wooden statues that stood by the door to the burial chamber. Below, pulleys hoist the king's second coffin from the shell of its outer container.

thieves had rampaged through that particular room, taking oils from vases, kicking objects aside, and opening coffers and boxes. Even so, 171 objects and pieces of furniture are listed in Carter's working diary — and many of these objects contained further, smaller items. Beyond the confused mass two splendid life-size statues of the king — each with flesh of black-lacquered wood, and each with clothing and headdress of gilded plaster — stood guarding a walled-up door. The second volume, describing the chamber that lay beyond and detailing the tomb's main focus, the royal burial, did not appear until 1926. The last volume, describing the contents of the Annex and Treasury, appeared in 1933, six years before Carter's death.

Besides lodging the only pharaoh ever discovered lying as he had been laid at the time of burial, the tomb contained almost all the objects with which Tutankhamen had been buried — and most of these were astonishingly well preserved. The only items of real importance that had been stolen were some golden statues from a shrine; the only items that had deteriorated markedly were the linen and the mummy itself, the latter through the excess of unguents poured over it at the time of burial. Otherwise much of the treasure seemed as though it had been placed there within living memory, not fourteen centuries before Christ. Flowers on funeral wreaths were easily identifiable; indeed, the presence of cornflower and mandrake blooms made it possible for a botanist to assert that Tutankhamen had been interred some time between the middle of March and the end of April.

The completeness and uniqueness of his find made Carter conscious of a responsibility to the future as

much as to the past; what had been so long preserved could so easily be harmed. To give preserving treatment to all the objects that required it, a field laboratory was established in the empty tomb of Seti II. The superb coffer found in the antechamber was one example of an object that needed such treatment. When discovered, the wood was in perfect condition except for a slight widening of the joints. At first it had seemed as if all that was required was to remove the dust and then to spray the coffer with a solution of celluloid in amyl-acetate to fix the gesso to the wood. But after about a month Carter's team of assistants was alarmed to discover that the transition from the close, rather humid atmosphere of the tomb to the dry air of the laboratory was causing the wood to shrink and the gesso to buckle. With considerable courage, Carter decided to apply melted paraffin wax to the exposed surfaces of the coffer — and his *ad hoc* solution worked. Other improvised methods were used on sandals, pendants, necklaces, and furniture.

Carter's devotion to the inanimate objects in his care had an ironic effect on the man whose money had facilitated their discovery: as a result of his colleague's sense of dedication, Carnarvon was never able to gaze on the pharaoh with whom his name would be eternally connected. However, he was present with Carter on February 17, 1923, when the sealed wall leading from the antechamber to the burial chamber was breached; by electric light the two men could see that a vast box-shaped shrine of gilded wood almost filled the room. Since it had not been pillaged, it could safely be surmised that it was the outer husk for the royal mummy. In fact, no less than four shrines, set

By the time of Tutankhamen's death in 1352 B.C., coffins in the shape of a mummy had replaced the simple rectangular chests previously used for royal burials. This practice served to reinforce the pharaoh's identification with Osiris, for the revered god of the underworld was commonly represented as a mummified king. Tutankhamen's second anthropoid coffin (below) — carved of gold-plated wood with a brilliant decorative patchwork of multicolored glass paste — is a superlative example of the goldsmith's art. The king's arms are folded across his chest; in his hands are the royal insignia, a flail and crook. Engraved in low relief on the sides of the coffin are the feathered wings of the goddesses Nekhbet and Wadjet, whose symbols — the vulture and cobra — crown the king's nemset *headdress. Each panel of a six-foot-high gilded wood shrine (left), constructed to house Tutankhamen's internal organs, is protected by the outstretched arms of a lovely free-standing golden goddess. Within the shrine a four-compartmented vessel, known as the canopic jar, held the viscera. Four identical alabaster busts of the king (left below) formed lids for the sacred container.*

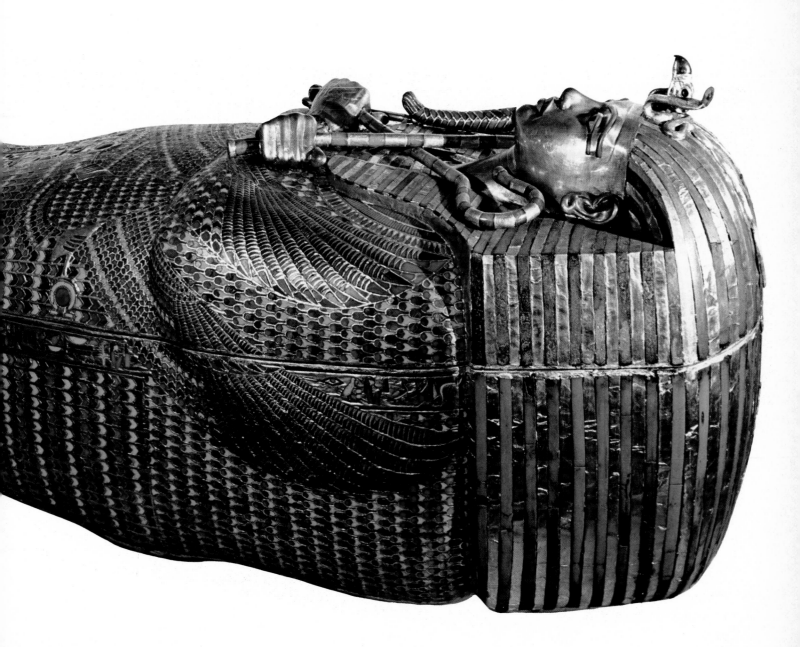

one within another like Chinese boxes, enfolded the pharaoh's red sandstone sarcophagus — itself the container of three man-shaped coffins, one inside another. At their heart, under a superb golden mask, lay Tutankhamen. But the last coffin, 2,448 ⅛ pounds of pure gold, was not opened until October 28, 1925, owing to the care required in the removal of the shrines and outer coffins. By this time Carnarvon was himself in the grave, his assassin a mosquito. Its random bite had turned septic and Carnarvon had died suddenly in Cairo on April 6, 1923.

Carnarvon's demise, so soon after his triumph — and coinciding with the simultaneous failure of every electric light in Cairo — was enough to establish the legend of a curse among the gullible. The legend was given new life when Carnarvon was quickly followed by two other Egyptologists who had entered the tomb: first the head of the Louvre's department of Egyptian antiquities, and then the assistant keeper of Egyptian antiquities at New York's Metropolitan Museum of Art. This was enough to set typewriters chattering, particularly as Carter had turned the press against him by giving exclusive coverage of his find to *The Times* of London. But the legend, when probed, proves to have little substance.

The features of the young king, as shown on his funerary mask of gold and lapis lazuli and as echoed on representations throughout the tomb, do not fit with the malevolence of a curse. Nor do the life stories of the many people who worked with Carter. On the contrary, these assistants enjoyed a longer than average life span; at least three of the more important were hale and active into their eighties. It might indeed be more apt to look for a pharaonic blessing. The welfare of a man's *ka* was linked by the ancient Egyptians to the survival of his name; those who passed a tomb were implored to recite the name of its occupant. The pharaoh's *ka* might thus approve of the men who had made Tutankhamen a household word the world over.

The mummy of the boy-king was left where it had been found, in the red sandstone sarcophagus, concealed in the outermost — and least valuable — of the three man-shaped coffins. The least of the Eighteenth Dynasty pharaohs thus enjoys a more dignified eternity than his predecessors and successors, whose faces are naked to the public gaze.

In February 1925, with world interest in Egyptology at its height and Tutankhamen's coffin still waiting to be opened, American archaeologist George Andrew Reisner was working in the Giza necropolis, the vast suburb of tombs that surrounds the pyramids. As with Carter in 1922, the chance discovery of an assistant — in this case the expedition's photographer — disclosed the long-sealed opening to an unsuspected tomb. It lay but a short distance to the east of the Great Pyramid, near the site of the original causeway.

To be buried in such a place, the person must have been important; to be buried so secretly, with no *mastaba* such as marked the streets of tombs to the west of the pyramid, indicated a mystery. The grave was in the form of a pit, a type frequently found in the Old Kingdom. After digging to a depth of more than eighty feet, the Americans came upon something very different from the curiosity shop of intact objects that Carter had seen when he put his eye to the hole in the second doorway of Tutankhamen's tomb. If

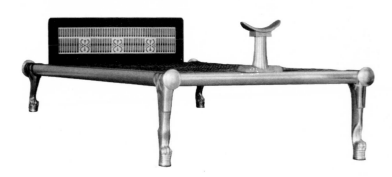

Carter's discovery had been remarkable for its excellent preservation, Reisner's was remarkable for its appearance of collapse and chaos. At first sight the only shapes amidst the shambles with discernible integrity were those of an alabaster sarcophagus and an alabaster canopic chest, a four-compartmented repository for those perishable parts that were removed from the body during the embalming process. A far more meticulous and painstaking examination than the one that had been required at Thebes was necessary if anything but a mass of sludge and debris were to be recovered; all wood, for example, had perished.

Such an examination, conducted more like a game of jackstraws than a dig, produced both disappointment and excitement. The sarcophagus was empty — and this fact was to pose a problem worthy of Agatha Christie. But it had unquestionably belonged to one of the most important women in Egyptian history, a queen who had died some twelve centuries before Tutankhamen was born. The woman was Hetep-Heres, the daughter of Huny, last king of the Third Dynasty founded by Zoser. By marrying Snofru, Hetep-Heres had probably ensured his claim to the throne as the founder of the Fourth Dynasty. The queen's son was none other than Cheops, builder of the **Great Pyramid** in whose shadow her tomb was dug.

But why, if the tomb furniture had been damaged only by time, not theft, was the sarcophagus empty? Not that all of the queen's body had perished: three of the four compartments in the canopic chest contained about five centimeters of a yellowish liquid, and upon analysis this was found to consist of a 3 per cent solution of natron in water. "In this," Reisner tells us, "lay the canopic packages which contained the entrails of the queen; all that has survived of the mortal remains of the mother of Cheops."

Reisner has left a conjectural interpretation of what may have happened. The queen's "house for eternity" had almost certainly been built during her lifetime, near the large pyramid of her husband, Snofru, at Dahshur. When she died, her body was probably embalmed at her son's mortuary workshop at Giza, then taken upriver for interment at Dahshur. But the vast works going on at Giza, the mobilization of labor for the construction of the Great Pyramid and its causeway, would have emptied the older necropolis of Snofru of all but a skeleton staff of priests. The sudden depopulation of Dahshur would have given thieves their opportunity to break into the queen's tomb and despoil her body. We know from Tutankhamen's tomb furnishings the quantity of gold that encased the royal mummy, as well as the variety and splendor of the ornaments and jewelry buried near it. Having stripped Hetep-Heres's mummy of what was most portable and precious, the thieves may have left the desiccated corpse to be gnawed at by jackals.

When the priests discovered what had happened, they were panic-stricken. A king who built so monumentally for himself would certainly punish heavily those responsible for endangering, by their negligence, his mother's hopes of immortality. Therefore some senior official — possibly Prince Hemiunu, chief minister to Cheops and Overseer of All the King's Works — may well have given Cheops a garbled account of what had happened: reporting the robbery, but suppressing the loss of the body. Cheops himself may have

suggested, or at least sanctioned, the proposal to rebury his mother in the protective shadow of his pyramid. A reverse procession, with an empty coffin, would have sailed downstream to Giza, where the causeway with its concealing walls would have enabled the priests to transport the queen's most personal treasures in secrecy to the hastily dug pit-grave. There the burial would have been completed in haste, without Cheops ever knowing that the tomb was a cenotaph.

If the body of Hetep-Heres has succumbed to mortality, evidence of her taste has survived. Thanks to the patient efforts of first Dows Dunham, an American, and then Ahmed Yusif, an Egyptian, the shambles has become a select collection in which only the wood is new. Its quality more than balances the quantity that astonished Carter and Carnarvon, for besides a supply of copper tools including razors, pots for cosmetics, and a toilet basin and ewer, the mother of Cheops took with her to eternity a superb but simple bed of gilded wood, two chairs (of which only one has been restored) with three entwined lotuses comprising the sides, and — most impressive of all — a long box covered with gold and inlaid with faience. This chest presumably contained the curtains for the bed; the masterly hieroglyphs on its sides — each ideogram a perfect form — enabled the archaeologists to attribute the tomb to Snofru's queen.

The style of this furniture is radically different from that discovered in Tutankhamen's tomb. It combines, in the words of Reisner himself, the exuberant fertility of invention that had characterized the Third Dynasty architecture of Imhotep with severe, simple lines of a more sober nature. The queen's surviving jewelry (and we may infer that the thieves took the best) cannot outflash Tutankhamen's complex pectorals and necklaces — but there is a remarkable series of bracelets so large they have been mistaken for anklets. They are ornamented with butterfly designs in lapis lazuli, turquoise, and carnelian.

At first sight, the restraint of the queen's taste seems hard to connect with the vast monument that is her tomb's neighbor and protector. But only on first sight. The mother of Cheops — the man who authorized the Grand Gallery, who chose severity of line rather than richness of ornament for his memorial — could only have delighted in a beauty that combined simplicity with power. The treasure of Hetep-Heres reflects in every detail the dawn period of Egyptian art, when each hieroglyph was a freshly fashioned picture and when what would become a style or even a habit was fresh and new. There was irony in the fact that it came alive, after more than four and a half thousand years, at the touch of men, American and Egyptian, living in the 1920's. For these children of the cluttered Victorian age, in their spats, trousers, and bow ties, the restraint and balance of Hetep-Heres's tomb furnishings embodied a cultural shock as sharp as the impact of primitive art on Picasso and his friends. The age whose architectural product was the movie palace, whose spiritual center was Hollywood-Babylon, could recognize a taste akin to its own in the lavish treasures of Tutankhamen — but it was rebuked by the simplicity of Hetep-Heres. The Africa of the third millennium before Christ had established standards rarely reached in the centuries since. But Reisner's discovery earned not a hundredth of the fame that troubled

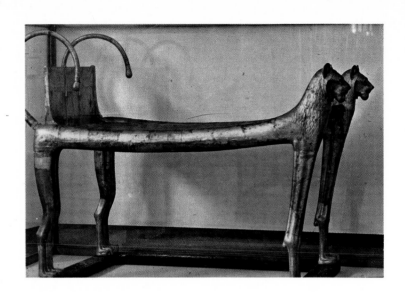 

Animal motifs predominate in the funerary equipment found in the antechamber of Tutankhamen's treasure house. The ornamental wooden chest below is decorated with a lively painting of the pharaoh, in a horse-drawn chariot, shooting deadly arrows at his enemies. The stuccoed and gilded funerary couch above is carved to resemble two animals' bodies; each terminates in the head of a fierce lioness (above right). One of the most beautiful objects from the king's tomb is the wooden throne with lions' heads supports (opposite), overlaid with gold, silver, semiprecious stones, and glass paste. Although Tutankhamen presided over the obliteration of his predecessor's heretical Aten worship, the exquisite back panel of this throne could have been designed for Akhenaten himself. It shows Tutankhamen seated on a cushioned chair, attended by his wife. In the rear, the sun disk showers beneficent rays upon the royal pair.

The Nineteenth Dynasty pharaoh Ramesses II
erected colossal edifices throughout Egypt. His most
grandiose memorials are two vast temples cut into the
sandstone cliffs at Abu Simbel. Twin pairs of seated
effigies of the king, each over sixty-five feet high,
form the façade of the larger temple (left). In order
to protect both structures from inundation as the
construction of the Aswan High Dam neared
completion in the 1960's, the temples were removed
from the rock piecemeal, hoisted to safe ground
(right) two hundred feet above their original site,
and painstakingly reassembled.

Carter, and to this day the room in Cairo Museum reserved for the treasures of Hetep-Heres is an uncrowded place, pleasant to visit.

The triumph of Carter and Carnarvon, acclaimed throughout the world, was received with misgivings only in Egypt. "In the course of an article on the Luxor discoveries," reported *The Egyptian Gazette* of December 16, 1922, "Maitre Fikri Abaza, a humorous Egyptian writer, remarks that not content with the occupation of the surface of Egypt, and with controlling the administration of the country, and interfering with the affairs of the living, the English want to extend the powers of their occupation to the underground world, and to control the belongings of the ancient forefathers of the people of this country, and to take a share of their mortal remains." As a result of nationalist pressure, it was decided that the whole of Tutankhamen's treasure should remain in Egypt. The nationalists, embittered by their struggle against a British occupation then forty years old, found it convenient to remember the depredations of nineteenth-century adventurers.

Egyptians had been conspicuous absentees from Egyptology and the administration of Egypt during the century and a quarter since Napoleon landed in Alexandria. Indeed, Egyptians were as rare among the pioneer Egyptologists honored in Cairo Museum as they were in the various governments that had ruled the country. Under the Turkish-speaking Khedive Ismail (1863–79), one Arab had risen — thanks to his talents for extorting taxes — to high authority; that Egyptian official, known as "the inspector," was casually murdered by the Khedive when his wealth, and

therefore his power, grew too great. After Britain and France deposed the bankrupt Ismail and replaced him with his weakling son, Tewfik Pasha, an Egyptian colonel named Arabi Pasha launched an abortive democratic revolution. The British used this "rebellion" as a pretext for bombarding Alexandria and landing an army of occupation on Egyptian soil. Although the British conceded a form of Egyptian independence in 1922, their army remained in the country.

While Saad Zaghlul Pasha, a fellah, was briefly premier, effective power remained divided between the British Embassy, a Macedonian monarchy, and a plutocracy consisting of Turks, Circassians, and resident aliens. But Zaghlul was soon evicted, and governments more representative of foreigners than Egyptians continued in power. It was July 23, 1952, thirty years after the finding of Tutankhamen's tomb, before Egyptians found themselves ruled by men of their own race. This was something they had not experienced since the death of Psammetichos III, the last pharaoh of the Twenty-sixth Dynasty, more than five hundred years before the birth of Christ.

The revolutionary junta that overthrew King Farouk in 1952 was dominated by Gamal Abdel Nasser, though for two years General Muhammad Naguib was allowed to act as its figurehead. The junta expressed, in an amateurish but passionate manner typical of soldiers, the consensus of 150 years of Egyptian struggle: their basic aims were the recovery of national independence and the restoration of national pride.

In this painful struggle against Mamelukes, Ottomans, the British, and a foreign dynasty, the monuments of ancient Egypt undoubtedly played an impor-

tant role, inspiring poets and politicians to glowing words. The leading Egyptian newspaper, founded in 1875, was named *Al-Ahram,* or *The Pyramids.* But throughout the nineteenth century almost the only Egyptian contribution to their history was through muscle power: they worked for foreign Egyptologists with hoe and shovel, just as they used their brawn to cut a man-made trough through the Isthmus of Suez.

In the twentieth century this situation changed; first Britain, then Europe and America, were forced to take account of Egyptian nationalism. On a gentle level, more and more young Egyptians studied Egyptology in the burgeoning universities of Cairo and Alexandria; novelists such as Tewfik al-Hakim (the favorite writer of the youthful Nasser) cited the achievements of the pharaohs as proof of the potential latent in Egyptians if only they could seize control of their fortunes. More violently, the incitement of the past inspired Egyptians of every class to sporadic outbursts against foreign occupation. The head of steam was so great by 1952 that the British found it impolitic to intervene on behalf of the monarchy. In 1954 they signed an agreement with the Egyptian republic under which they evacuated their bases, reserving the right to return if an outside power attacked the Arab states or Turkey. By having disastrous second thoughts in 1956 and attacking Egypt in collusion with Israel and France — and without the knowledge or approval of the United States — Britain forfeited even this residual right.

The reason for the attack on Egypt was Nasser's nationalization of the Suez Canal in July 1956. He had taken this step because of an Anglo-American rebuff to the scheme that for him symbolized his revolution:

a High Dam at Aswan. The grandeur of this scheme undoubtedly owed much to the nagging presence of the gigantic pyramids. For the challenge of having antiquity's greatest monuments on their modern skyline made it certain that Egyptians would think in larger terms than nationalists in countries with lesser pasts. Despite their comparatively small numbers, Egyptians saw their cultural heritage as equal with that of China or India. They often quoted Napoleon's St. Helena dictum — "Egypt is the most important country" — although in a different sense from that of the emperor of the French. To Napoleon, and later to the British, Egypt was important to control because of its strategic position. The young revolutionaries grouped around Nasser had another viewpoint: they would use Egypt's perilous centrality — the factor that had led to her continual enslavement — to make her independent and free.

Without a certain gigantism of the imagination the High Dam would have been impossible. It was achieved by a resolute determination to take aid from any source that would offer it — and after Britain and the United States refused, Soviet assistance was accepted.

This dam, advertised as requiring seventeen times more rock than the Great Pyramid, is creating a man-made lake destined to be bigger than Lebanon. This liking for sheer size made the rock temples of Abu Simbel, threatened by the rising waters of Lake Nasser, favorites of the revolution.

Four schemes were proposed whereby these could be saved for posterity. A French scheme envisaged a subsidiary dam three hundred feet high to hold back the waters of the lake and allow the temples to survive

133

Imperious masters of the horizon, the triple wonders of ancient Egypt — the pyramids of Mycerinus, Chephren, and Cheops — unite to form an abstract image in defiance of time.

as they were, although in a pit below water level. An Italian scheme proposed cutting away the temples from the rock, enclosing them in huge concrete boxes reinforced with steel and then raising them on 650 synchronized jacks a sixteenth of an inch at a time. When the jacks were fully extended, concrete pillars would replace them; the jacking operation would then be repeated as often as was required to raise the temples above the danger line. A third, British scheme was the most imaginative and the least acceptable. This was to allow the temples to be submerged but to ward off the muddy waters of the Nile with a membrane dam a foot thick. Visitors would be able to descend by observation car and enter the floodlit aquarium through viewing passages. The scheme that was finally approved was a Swedish one. In an unprecedented feat of engineering, the temples of Ramesses II and his wife, Nefertary (her name means "Beautiful Companion"), were cut from the ferruginous sandstone in blocks. These blocks were then hauled to the top of the cliff, where they were reassembled to overlook the waters of Lake Nasser as they had overlooked the upper Nile in centuries past.

Thus revolutionary Egypt retains, from one end to another, gigantic mentors to remind Egyptians — and for that matter all humanity — that the past is also present and to be. Less spectacular but no less powerful are the gentler, smaller objects created by past genius, the works of sculptor, painter, and craftsman. Given their time, these too may stimulate a jaded world, an overpoliticized generation, to the creation of that calm beauty without which even the largest dam gives fertility and power in vain.

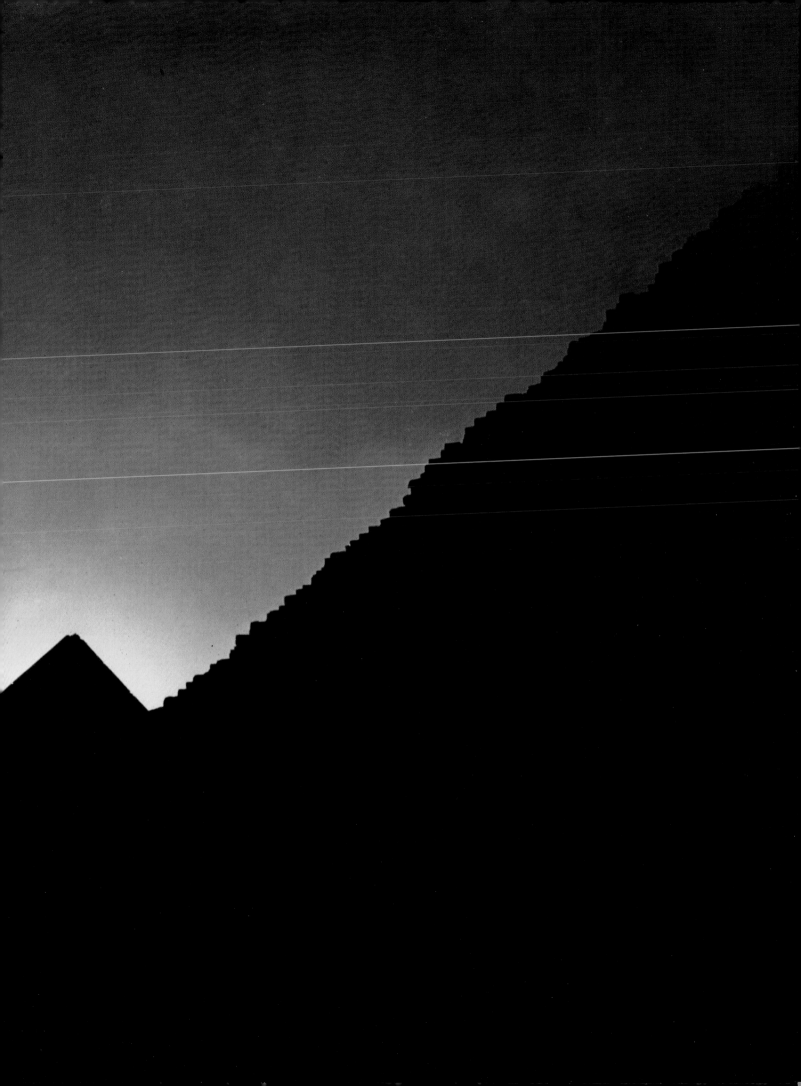

THE PYRAMIDS
AND SPHINX
IN LITERATURE

The earliest — and still perhaps the best — commentary on ancient Egyptian civilization dates from the fifth century B.C. Herodotus, author of that account, was as distant in time from the pyramid builders as twentieth-century man is from the Greek historian. In repeating as fact the somewhat fanciful stories of the dragomans he encountered in Egypt, the "father of history" helped perpetuate innumerable inaccuracies concerning the pyramids.

Cheops succeeded to the throne, and plunged into all manner of wickedness. He closed the temples, and forbade the Egyptians to offer sacrifice, compelling them instead to labour, one and all, in his service. Some were required to drag blocks of stone down to the Nile from the quarries in the Arabian range of hills; others received the blocks after they had been conveyed in boats across the river, and drew them to the range of hills called the Libyan. A hundred thousand men laboured constantly, and were relieved every three months by a fresh lot. It took ten years' oppression of the people to make the causeway for the conveyance of the stones, a work not much inferior, in my judgment, to the pyramid itself. This causeway is five furlongs in length, ten fathoms wide, and in height, at the highest part, eight fathoms. It is built of polished stone, and is covered with carvings of animals. To make it took ten years, as I said — or rather to make the causeway, the works on the mound where the pyramid stands, and the underground chambers, which Cheops intended as vaults for his own use: these last were built on a sort of island, surrounded by water introduced from the Nile by a canal. The Pyramid itself was twenty years in building. It is a square, eight hundred feet each way, and the height the same, built entirely of polished stone, fitted together with the utmost care. The stones of which it is composed are none of them less than thirty feet in length.

The pyramid was built in steps, battlement-wise, as it is called, or, according to others, altar-wise. After laying the stones for the base, they raised the remaining stones to their places by means of machines formed of short wooden planks. The first machine raised them from the ground to the top of the first step. On this there was another machine, which received the stone upon its arrival, and conveyed it to the second step, whence a third machine advanced it still higher. Either they had as many machines as there were steps in the pyramid, or possibly they had but a single machine, which, being easily moved, was transferred from tier to tier as the stone rose — both accounts are given, and therefore I mention both. The upper portion of the pyramid was finished first, then the middle, and finally the part which was lowest and nearest the ground. There is an inscription in Egyptian characters on the pyramid which records the quantity of radishes, onions, and garlick consumed by the labourers who constructed it; and I perfectly well remember that the interpreter who read the writing to me said that the money expended in this way was 1600 talents of silver. If this then is a true record, what a vast sum must have been spent on the iron tools used in the work, and on the feeding and clothing of the labourers, considering the length of time the work lasted, which has already been stated, and the additional time — no small space, I imagine — which must have been occupied by the quarrying of the stones, their conveyance, and the formation of the underground apartments.

HERODOTUS
The Histories, c. 455 B.C.

Much more was known about the pyramids at Giza by the first century A.D., *when Pliny the Elder included a brief history of Egypt in his massive opus* Natural History. *Yet even as conscientious a scholar as Pliny reported an outlandish tale about the origin of the third pyramid. This Roman historian was so inordinately devoted to his craft that he succumbed to asphyxiation while attempting to make firsthand observations of the eruption of Mount Vesuvius.*

We must make some mention, . . . however cursorily, of the Pyramids of Egypt, so many idle and frivolous pieces of ostentation of their resources, on the part of the monarchs of that country. Indeed, it is asserted by most persons, that the only motive for constructing them, was either a determination not to leave their treasures to their successors or to rivals that might be plotting to supplant them, or to prevent the lower classes from remaining unoccupied. There was great vanity displayed by these men in constructions of this description, and there are still the remains of many of them in an unfinished state. . . .

The . . . three pyramids, the renown of which has filled the whole earth, and which are conspicuous from every quarter to persons navigating the river, are situate on the African side of it, upon a rocky sterile elevation. They lie between the city of Memphis and what we have mentioned as the Delta, within four miles of the river, and seven miles and a-half from Memphis, near a village known as Busiris, the people of which are in the habit of ascending them. . . .

In front of these pyramids is the Sphinx, a still more wondrous object of art, but one upon which silence has been observed, as it is looked upon as a divinity by the people of the neighbourhood. It is their belief that King Harmais was buried in it, and they will have it that it was brought there from a distance. The truth is, however, that it was hewn from the solid rock; and, from a feeling of veneration, the face of the monster is coloured red. The circumference of the head, measured round the forehead, is one hundred and two feet, the length of the feet being one hundred and forty-three, and the height, from the belly to the summit of the asp on the head, sixty-two.

The largest Pyramid is built of stone quarried in Arabia: three hundred and sixty thousand men, it is said, were employed upon it twenty years, and the three were completed in seventy-eight years and four months. They are described by [many] writers. . . . These authors, however, are disagreed as to the persons by whom they were constructed; accident having, with very considerable justice, consigned to oblivion the names of those who erected such stupendous memorials of their vanity. Some of these writers inform us that fifteen hundred talents were expended upon radishes, garlic, and onions alone.

The largest Pyramid occupies seven jugera of ground, and the four angles are equidistant, the face of each side being eight hundred and thirty-three feet in length. The total height from the ground to the summit is seven hundred and twenty-five feet, and the platform on the summit is sixteen and a-half in circuit. Of the second Pyramid, the faces of the four sides are each seven hundred and fifty-seven feet and a-half in length. The third is smaller than the others, but far more prepossessing in appearance: it is built of AEthiopian stone, and the face between the four corners is three hundred and sixty-three feet in extent. In the vicinity of these erections, there are no vestiges of any buildings left. Far and wide there is nothing but sand to be seen, of a grain somewhat like a lentil in appearance, similar to that of the greater part of Africa, in fact.

The most difficult problem is, to know how the materials for construction could possibly be carried to so vast a height. According to some authorities, as the building gradually advanced, they heaped up against it vast mounds of nitre and salt; which piles were melted after its completion, by introducing beneath them the waters of the river. Others, again, maintain, that bridges were constructed, of bricks of clay, and that, when the pyramid was completed, these bricks were distributed for erecting the houses of private individuals. For the level of the river, they say, being so much lower, water could never by any possibility have been brought there by the medium of canals. In the interior of the largest Pyramid there is a well, eighty-six cubits deep, which communicates with the river, it is thought. The method of ascertaining the height of the Pyramids and all other similar edifices was discovered by Thales of Miletus; he measuring the shadow at the hour of the day at which it is equal in length to the body projecting it.

Such are the marvellous Pyramids; but the crowning marvel of all is, that the smallest, but most admired of them — that we may feel no surprise at the opulence of the kings — was built by Rhodopis, a courtesan! This woman was once the fellow-slave of AEsopus the philosopher and fabulist, and the sharer of his bed; but what is much more surprising is, that a courtesan should have been enabled, by her vocation, to amass such enormous wealth.

> PLINY THE ELDER
> *Natural History*, 77 A.D.

Egypt had been a province of Islam for more than five hundred years by the time Abdul Latif traveled there in the twelfth century. The eminent Iraqi physician also visited Greece, Turkey, and Syria — but nothing excited his keen scientific admiration so much as the pyramids and Sphinx.

A TOURIST'S DELIGHT

Of all the countries I have visited or known by report of others, there are not any can compare with Egypt for its antiquities. I will say only about the wonders that I saw.

The pyramids are one of the wonders. They have engaged the attention of a multitude of writers who have given in their works the description and dimensions of these edifices. . . .

As to those pyramids, the object of so many recitals, to which I shall now advert, pyramids distinguished above the rest, the superior size of which excites admiration: the number of them is three, and they stand in a line at Gizeh in front of Fostat, at a short distance apart, their angles pointing to each other and towards the east. Two of these pyramids are of enormous dimensions, and the same size. The poets who have described them have given the rein to that enthusiasm they are so well calculated to inspire. They compare them to two immense breasts rising from the bosom of Egypt. They are very near to each other, and are built of white stone.

The third one, a fourth part less than the others, is of red granite marked with points and so extremely hard that iron takes a long time, with difficulty, to make an impression on it. The last one appears small compared with the other two, but viewed at a short distance and to the exclusion of these it excites in the imagination a singular oppression, and cannot be contemplated without painfully affecting the sight.

The shape chosen for the pyramids and their solidity are alike admirable. To their form is owing the advantage of their having resisted the attack of centuries: they stayed continuously against time, and time patiently waits on them. In fact, after mature reflection on the structure of the pyramids one is forced to acknowledge the combination of efforts of the most intelligent men, an exhaustion of the genius of the most subtle, that the most enlightened minds exercised with profusion in favour of these edifices all the talents they possessed, and that the most learned theory of geometry called forth the whole of its resources to show in these wonders the utmost term of human ability. We may likewise affirm that these structures hold discourse with us even in the present day respecting those who were their founders, teach us their history in a manner intelligible to all, relate their progress in the sciences and the excellence of their genius, and in short, effectually describe their life and news. . . .

We were told that in a neighbouring village there were people accustomed to mount to the summit of the pyramids, and who effected it without difficulty. We sent for one of these men, who for a trifle ascended one of the pyramids in the same manner that and even quicker than we should a staircase, and without taking off his shoes or his dress which was very wide. . . .

One of these pyramids is opened and has an entrance by which the interior may be penetrated. This opening leads by narrow passages to conduits extending to a great depth to wells and precipices, according to the testimony of individuals bold enough to enter; for many, excited by desperate cupidity and by delusory expectations, have ventured into the interior of this building. They explored its deepest cavities, and finally arrived at a spot beyond which it is impossible to advance. As for the passage the most frequented and that which is commonly followed, it is by a slope which leads towards the upper part of the pyramid where is a square chamber containing a sarcophagus of stone. The opening by which the pyramid is now entered is not the door formed at the period of its erection, but a hole excavated with great trouble and directed by chance, the making of which is ascribed to the Caliph Mamoun [ninth century A.D.].

Most of our company entered this opening and ascended to the chamber in the upper part of the pyramid. On their return they talked of the wonderful things they had seen, that the passage was so full of bats and their ordure as to be almost closed, that the bats were as large as pigeons, and that in the upper part openings were seen and windows, designed apparently for the admission of air and light.

On a second visit I myself, with several others, entered the interior conduit, and penetrated about two-thirds of its length, but losing consciousness owing to the terror I experienced in the ascent, I returned, half dead.

These pyramids are built of large stones between 10 and 20 cubits long by a breadth and thickness each of 2 to 3 cubits; but most especially worthy of admiration is the extreme nicety with which these stones are fashioned and disposed one above the other. The courses fit so exactly that not even a needle or a single hair can be thrust between the joints. They are cemented together by a mortar which forms a layer the thickness of a leaf of paper. With the composition of this mortar I am totally unacquainted. The stones are covered with writing in those ancient characters of which the meaning is now unknown. I have met with no-one in Egypt who either knew it himself or had ever heard of any person by whom it was comprehended. So numerous are these inscriptions that were only those to be copied which are found on the surface of these two pyramids, they would fill about ten thousand pages. . . .

A sensible man enquiring of me as to what, of all I had seen in Egypt, had most excited my admiration, I answered: "The nicety of proportion in the head of the Sphinx". In fact, between the different parts of this head, the nose, for example, the eyes, and the ears, the same proportion is remarked as is observed by nature in her works. Thus, the nose of a child is suitable to its stature, and proportioned to the rest of its frame, while if it belonged to the face of a full-grown man it would be reckoned a deformity. The nose of a grown man on the visage of a child would equally be a disfigurement. The same holds good with respect to all the other members. There are none but should have a certain form and dimension in order to bear relation to such and such a face, and where these proportions are not observed, the face is spoiled. Hence the wonder that in a face of such colossal size the sculptor should have been able to preserve the exact proportion of every part, seeing that nature presented him with no model of a similar colossus or any at all comparable.

ABDUL LATIF
The Eastern Key, c. 1200

When Englishman George Sandys visited Egypt in 1610, the country was still recovering from the devastating Ottoman Turk conquest a century earlier. Yet Sandys, a prominent poet who settled in Virginia and later represented the colony in a charter dispute with England, had no trouble reaching his destination, "Full West of the Citie."

Full West of the Citie, close upon those deserts, aloft on a rocky levell adjoyning to the valley, stands those three Pyramides (the barbarous monuments of prodigality and vain-glory) so universally celebrated. The name is derived from a flame of fire, in regard to their shape: broad below, and sharpe above, like a pointed Diamond. . . . The greatest of the three, and chiefe of the worlds seven wonders, being square at the bottome, is supposed to take up eight acres of ground. Each square being 300 single paces in length, the square at the top, consisting of three stones onely, yet large enough for threescore to stand upon: ascended by two hundred fifty five steps, each step above three feet high, of a breadth proportionable. No stone so little throughout the whole, as to be drawne by our carriages; yet were these hewne out of the Trojan mountaines, far off in Arabia. . . . A wonder how conveyed hither: how so mounted, a greater. . . .

. . . [The Great Pyramid] hath bene too great a morsell for time to devoure; having stood, as may be probably conjectured, about three thousand and two hundred yeares: and now rather old than ruinous: yet the North side most worne, by reason of the humidity of the Northerne wind, which here is the moistest. The top at length we ascended with many pauses and much difficulty; from whence with delighted eyes we beheld that soveraigne of streames [the Nile], and most excellent of countries. Southward and neare hand the Mummes: afar off divers huge Pyramides; each of which, were this away, might supply the repute of a wonder. During a great part of the day it

casteth no shadow on the earth, but is at once illuminated on all sides. Descending againe, on the East side, below, from each corner equally distant, we approched the entrance, seeming heretofore to have bene closed up, or so intended, both by the place it selfe, and conveyances within. Into this our Janissaries discharged their harquebuses, lest some should have skulkt within to have done us a mischiefe: and guarded the mouth whilst we entred, for feare of the wilde Arabs. To take the better footing we put off our shooes, and most of our apparell: foretold of the heat within, not inferior to a stove. Our guide (a Moore) went foremost: every one of us with our lights in our hands. A most dreadfull passage, and no lesse cumbersome; not above a yard in breadth, and foure feete in height: each stone containing that measure. So that always stooping, and sometimes creeping, by reason of the rubbidge [rubbish], we descended (not by staires, but as downe the steepe of a hill,) a hundred feete: where the place for a little circuite enlarged; and the fearefull descent continued, which they say none ever durst attempt any farther. Save that a Basha of Cairo, curious to search into the secrets thereof, caused divers condemned persons to undertake the performance; well stored with lights and other provision: and that some of them ascended againe well-nigh thirty miles off in the Deserts. A fable devised onely to beget wonder.

But others have written, that at the bottome there is a spacious pit, eightie and six cubits deepe, filled at the overflow by concealed conduits: in the middst a little Island, and on that a tombe containing the body of Cheops, a King of Egypt, and the builder of this Pyramid: which with the truth hath a greater affinity. For since I have bene told by one out of his owne experience, that in the uttermost depth there is a large square place (though without water) into which he was led by another entry opening to the South, known but unto few (that now open being shut by some order) and came up at this place. A turning on the right hand leadeth into a little roome: which by reason of the noysome vapour and uneasie passage we refused to enter. Clambering over the mouth of the aforesaid dungeon, we ascended as upon the bow of an arch, the way no larger than the former, about a hundred and twenty feete. Here we passed through a long entry which led directly forward: so low, that it tooke even from us that uneasie benefit of stooping. Which brought us into a little roome with a compact rooffe, more long than broad, of polished marble, whose grave-like smell, halfe-full of rubbidge forced our quicke returne. Climbing also over this entrance, we ascended as before, about an hundred and twenty feete higher. This entry being of an exceeding height, yet no broader from side to side than a man may fathome, benched on each side, and closed above with admirable architecture, the marble so great, and so cunningly joined, as if it had bene hewne through the living rocke. At the top we entred into a goodly chamber, twenty foote wide, and forty in length: the rooffe of a marvellous height; and the stones so great, . . . all of well wrought Theban marble. Athwart the roome at the upper end there standeth a tombe: uncovered, empty, and all of one stone: breast high, seven feete in length, not foure in breadth, and sounding like a bell. In this no doubt lay the body of the builder. They erecting such costly monuments, not onely out of a vaine ostentation: but being of opinion, that after the dissolution of the flesh the soul should survive; and when thirty six thousand yeares were expired, againe be joined unto the selfesame body.

GEORGE SANDYS
A Relation of a Journey, 1610

Alexandre Dumas — known as Dumas père to distinguish him from his equally famous son — was an astonishingly prolific writer who produced nearly three hundred plays and novels during his lifetime. The energetic author of The Three Musketeers *and* The Count of Monte Cristo *tackled the challenge of the pyramids at Giza with as much gusto as a swashbuckling hero out of one of his own historical romances.*

We resolved to visit the Pyramids the next day, pass over the battle ground and return by Gizeh. At day-break our beasts were at the door; we mounted, and proved their good qualities by arriving at Boulac in ten minutes. We here crossed the Nile. . . . but our survey was short; for everything here was for association and thought, and nothing for description.

On our landing, the first Pyramid seemed to be within a stone's throw; yet owing to the actual distance, and to the character of the intervening sand, in which our beasts sunk to their knees at every step, nearly five hours were occupied in reaching it.

The largest Pyramid, and the one we preferred to ascend, rests on a base six hundred and ninety feet long, and appears, from below, slightly sloping at its summit. It is built of large stones, placed on each other in receding tiers, and has the appearance, on its sides, of a gigantic stair-case, each step of which is about four feet high and ten inches broad. The ascent appeared, at first, difficult, if not impossible; but Mohammed attacked an angle, sprang with address up the first step and invited us to follow him, as if it were the easiest thing in the world. Still, however slight might be the pleasure of clambering upwards more than four hundred feet under a broiling sun, and with a dazzling reflection in our eyes from the stones to which we must cling like lizards, we were ashamed to stay behind.

This was Mayer's turn to triumph. Accustomed, in his vocation, to run up the rigging of his ship, he mounted from ledge to ledge like a goat in a frolic. We followed as we best could; and, after twenty minutes of hard labour, we reached the top without any nails on our fingers or skin on our knees. Our next care, — and we were immediately impressed with it, — was to descend: for the little fat which this Egyptian sun had left on our bones, was fast melting away. However, fat or no fat, I resolved to turn my labour to some account, and have a view of the landscape before I descended. Turning my back on Cairo, the immense forest of palms that covers the site of Memphis was on my left; beyond the forest stood the Pyramids of Sakkarah; beyond these lay the Desert; in front, the Desert; on my right, the Desert: in short, a vast plain, of the colour of fire, unvaried save by here and there a sand-hill, now heaped up by the wind, to be, by the wind, levelled again the next hour. Facing about, there lay Egypt, i.e. the Nile, gliding through an emerald-valley; then Cairo, a living city, between Fostat and the Tombs of the Caliphs, her two dead sisters: and beyond the Tombs of the Caliphs, the sterile range of the Mokattan mountains enclosing the landscape with granite walls.

I stepped around the platform, which appeared to extend thirty or thirty-five feet. Some enormous stones were lying about, like peaks torn from the crest of a mountain. These are covered with names, among which are some, still legible, of those belonging to the Egyptian expedition. Near these I saw *Charles Nodier* and *Chateaubriand,* inscribed by Mr. Taylor on a previous visit.

I now looked at the foot of the Pyramid, where stood our asses and drivers, like beetles and ants. I attempted to throw a stone to them, but, with all my efforts, I could not cast it clear of the base: it fell on the side, and bounded along to the ground.

The latter motion of this stone struck me as typical of my own descent, which process now presented a difficulty unlike, and yet not inferior to that of our ascent. The width of the steps was so disproportioned to their height, that each upper edge overhung or rather hid the step that next succeeded it; and the only method of reaching the ground seemed to be a *sheer slide* in a sitting posture. Luckily, one thinks twice before attempting such a *glissade*. On stepping to the very verge of the first stone, the second became visible; and a succession of well graduated jumps accomplished the task safely. Still, I would recommend all persons liable to vertigo, to refrain from ascending the Pyramids.

When I reached the ground, I threw myself on the sand, dying with heat and thirst. I had not thought of the latter before, so much was I occupied with other matters. Mohammed discoursed very sagely about the necessity of drinking but little at a time; and I replied by seizing the bottle from his hand and draining it at a draught. Hunger was the next affection; and as all were of one mind on this point, breakfast was ordered, instanter. The sumpter-ass was marched up, and we observed with satisfaction that no accident had happened to its freight.

We made the circuit of the Pyramid to find a shade. But the sun was in its zenith, and blazed equally on the four sides of the tomb of Cheops. We could not find a spot where it was possible to remain more than five minutes without becoming crazy. At this juncture, one of our Arabs pointed out the entrance into the Pyramid, on the north side, and about one-third of the distance to the top. This sombre orifice, through which one might imagine that the Colossus breathed, seemed to promise shade and coolness; and, despite our exhaustion, we mounted with some alacrity to reach it. In five minutes we were in a dining-room, which, if not very commodious, was sufficiently cool.

After our breakfast, we ordered torches to explore the inside of the Pyramid. The entrance is by a square corridor about three feet in dimension, descending at an angle of forty-five degrees. As we receded from the entrance, the heat rapidly diminished; but the air, thickened by the smoke of the torches, and mixed with the impalpable dust raised by our motion, was very difficult to breathe. The two chambers, within, are known as the King's room and the Queen's room: in the former is a sarcophagus of granite, with the cover broken; the latter is empty.

We left these chambers (containing nothing to repay the trouble of a visit) to salute her highness, the Sphinx. It is nearer to the Nile than the Pyramids by a few hundred yards; and may be called the gigantic dog that watches this granite flock. With the assistance of my Arabs, I succeeded in mounting its back, and from its back to its head, which was no easy job. Mayer immediately followed. I then slipped down to the shoulders of the Colossus, and from there to the ground, and began to sketch. Mayer, standing on its ear, served for its plume, and also supplied me with a scale of proportion.

ALEXANDRE DUMAS
Impressions of Travel, in Egypt and Arabia, 1830

Harriet Martineau, a successful English novelist as well as an eccentric and inde-
pendent thinker, challenged nineteenth-century views on religion, economics, and
politics. Undaunted by her age, her chronic deafness, or the conventional restric-
tions placed upon members of her sex, she journeyed to Egypt's most famous
monuments — the pyramids and Sphinx — in 1846. Ironically, Miss Martineau's
practical advice to prospective travelers hoping to duplicate her adventure reveals
her traditional Victorian upbringing.

One . . . anecdote, otherwise too personal for print, will show how engrossing is the interest of the Pyramid on the spot. — The most precious articles
of property I had with me abroad were two ear-trumpets, because, in case of
accident happening to them, I could not supply the loss. I was unwilling to
carry my trumpet up the Pyramid, — knocking against the stones while I
wanted my hands for climbing. So I left it below, in the hands of a trusty
Arab. When I joined my party at the top of the Pyramid, I never remembered
my trumpet: nor did they: and we talked as usual, during the forty minutes
we were there, without my ever missing it. — When I came down, I never
thought of it: and I explored the inside, came out and lunched, and still
never thought of my trumpet, till, at the end of three hours and a half from
my parting with it, I saw it in the hands of the Arab, and was reminded of the
astonishing fact that I had heard as well without it as with it, all that time.
Such a thing never happened before, and probably never will again: and a
stronger proof could not be offered of the engrossing interest of a visit to the
Pyramid. . . .

On looking up, it was not the magnitude of the Pyramid which made me
think it scarcely possible to achieve the ascent; but the unrelieved succession, — almost infinite, — of bright yellow steps; a most fatiguing image! —
Three strong and respectable-looking Arabs now took me in charge. One of
them, seeing me pinning up my gown in front, that I might not stumble over
it, gave me his services as lady's-maid. He turned up my gown all round, and
tied it in a most squeezing knot, which lasted all through the enterprise. We
set out from the north-east corner. By far the most formidable part of the
ascent was the first six or eight blocks. If it went on to the top thus broken
and precipitous, the ascent would, I felt, be impossible. Already, it was disagreeable to look down, and I was much out of breath. One of my Arabs
carried a substantial camp-stool, which had been given me in London with a
view to this very adventure, — that it might divide the higher steps, — some
of which, being four feet high, seem impracticable enough beforehand. But
I found it better to trust to the strong and steady lifting of the Arabs in such
places, and, above every thing, not to stop at all, if possible; or, if one must
stop for breath, to stand with one's face to the Pyramid. I am sure the guides
are right in taking people quickly. The height is not so great, in itself: it is
the way in which it is reached that is trying to look back upon. It is trying
to some heads to sit on a narrow ledge, and see a dazzling succession of such
ledges for two or three hundred feet below; and there, a crowd of diminutive
people looking up, to see whether one is coming bobbing down all that vast
staircase. I stopped for a few seconds two or three times, at good broad corners
or ledges. — When I left the angle, and found myself ascending the side, the
chief difficulty was over; and I cannot say that the fatigue was at all formidable. The greater part of one's weight is lifted by the Arabs at each arm;
and when one comes to a four feet step, or a broken ledge, there is a third

Arab behind. When we arrived at a sort of recess, broken in the angle, my guides sported two of their English words, crying out "Half-way!" with great glee. The last half was easier than the first; and I felt, what proved to be true, that both must be easier than the coming down. I arrived second, and was kindly welcomed to that extraordinary spot by Mr. E. Mrs. Y. appeared presently after; and lastly, Mr. Y.; — all in good spirits.

I was agreeably surprised to find at the top, besides blocks standing up which gave us some shade, a roomy and even platform, where we might sit and write, and gaze abroad, and enjoy ourselves, without even seeing over the edge, unless we wished it. There was only the lightest possible breeze, just enough to fan our faces, without disturbing us. The reason of our ascending the Pyramid first, before going into it, was that we might take advantage of an hour of calm, and avoid the inconvenience of the wind which might spring up at noon. And most fortunate we were in our weather. . . .

The descent was fatiguing; but not at all alarming. Between stepping, jumping, and sliding, with full reliance on the strength and care of the guides, the descent may be easily accomplished in ten minutes; — as far, that is, as the height of the entrance to the Pyramid, which is some way from the bottom. . . . I joined my party at the beautiful entrance to the Pyramid, where a large assemblage of Arabs was ranged on the rising stones opposite to us, like a hill-side congregation waiting for the preacher.

I resolved that morning not to be induced by any pleasure or triumph of the hour to tell people that it is very easy to go up and into the Pyramid. To determined and practised people it is easy; but not, probably, to the majority. I would not recommend any one to do it of whose nerve I was not sure. To the tranquil, the inside of the Pyramid is sufficiently airy and cool for the need of the hour. But it is a dreadful place in which to be seized with a panic: and no woman should go who cannot trust herself to put down panic by reason. There is absolutely nothing to fear but from one's self; no danger of bad falls, or of going astray, or of being stifled. The passages are slippery: but there are plenty of notches; and a fall could hardly be danger-ous, — unless at one place, — the entrance upon the passage to the King's Chamber. We knew beforehand that there were air passages from that chamber to the outside; and when I walked about before examining the place, and questioned my senses, I was surprised to find how little oppressive heat, and how much air there really was. The one danger is from the im-pression upon the senses of the solidity and vastness of the stone structure in such darkness. Almost any nerves may be excused for giving way under the sight of that passage and that chamber; — the whole, even the roof, being constructed of blocks of dark granite, so joined as that the edge of a penknife could not be inserted between them. The passage runs up, a steep inclined plane, with its lines on either hand, and its notches in front, retiring almost to a vanishing point, other grooves and projections high up the side walls apparently coming down to the same vanishing point, and all closed in by the ponderous ceiling, at such a height as to be well nigh lost in gloom. The torches of the Arabs glare near the eye, and perplex the vision by their fitful shining on the granite walls; and at the same time, the lights in advance or far behind are like waving glow-worm sparks. There is nothing else like it; — no catacomb or cavern in the world; there never was, and surely there never will be. . . . The fantastic character of its walls and roofs takes off from the impression of its vastness and gloom. Here, the symmetry and finish so deepen the gloom as to make this seem like a fit prison-house for fallen angels. Notwithstanding the plain view we obtained in the chamber of the enormous longitudinal blocks of the ceiling, the impression was less tremendous than in the descending passage, from the inferior vastness. — There is nothing but the structure itself to be seen, except the sarcophagus near one end. It is sadly broken: but it still rings like a bell, when struck on the side. — The granite is blackened by time; but its grain is seen where it has been chipped by those who were in search of the air-holes. — The prodigious portcullises of granite in the passage were more visible to us in going down than in ascending: and how they came there was an oppressive speculation in itself....

And now the time was come for visiting the Sphinx. What a monstrous idea was it from which this monster sprang! True as I think Abdallatif's [Abdul Latif] account of it, and just as is his admiration, I feel that a stranger either does not see the Sphinx at all, or he sees it as a nightmare. When we first passed it, I saw it only as a strange looking rock; an oversight which could not have occurred in the olden time, when the head bore the royal helmet or the ram's horns. Now I was half-afraid of it. The full serene gaze of its round face, rendered ugly by the loss of the nose, which was a very handsome feature of the old Egyptian face; — this full gaze, and the stony calm of its attitude almost turn one to stone. So life-like, — so huge, — so monstrous, — it is really a fearful spectacle. I saw a man sitting in a fold of the neck, — as a fly might settle on a horse's mane. In that crease he reposed, while far over his head extended the vast penthouse of the jaw; and above that, the dressed hair on either side the face, — each bunch a mass of stone which might crush a dwelling house.... Fancy the long well-opened eyes ... eyes which have gazed unwinking into vacancy, while mighty Pharaohs, and Hebrew law-givers, and Persian princes, and Greek philosophers, and Anthony with Cleopatra by his side, and Christian anchorites, and Arab warriors, and European men of science, have been brought hither in succession by the unpausing ages to look up into those eyes, — so full of meaning, though so fixed! We have here a record of the Egyptian complexion, or of the Egyptians' own notion of it, as well as of the characteristic features of the race. There is red paint on the face, of the same tint as the complexions in the tombs. The face is (supposing the nose restored) much like the Berber countenance. The long mild eye, the thick, but not protuberant lips, ... and the projecting jaw, with the intelligent, gentle expression of the whole face, are very like what one sees in Nubia at every village. That man sitting in the fold of the neck was a happy accident. It enabled one to estimate proportions, when looking up from below: and to learn how it was that religious processions marched up between its paws to the temple sheltered by its breast. I could see how the sanctuary and altar of sacrifice might very well stand there, so towered over by the neck and head as that the savour of the sacrifices might rise straight up into its nostrils. The granite tablet above this altar is visible, peeping out of the sand in the hollow. The ridge of the back is above ground, and I walked along it from the neck to the root of the tail. — If only the paws could be kept uncovered, it would much improve our conception of this strange work, — perhaps, as my journal observes, the strangest object I ever saw.

HARRIET MARTINEAU
Eastern Life, Present and Past, 1846

One less-than-awestruck visitor to the monuments of ancient Egypt was the nineteenth-century English novelist and satirist William M. Thackeray. Writing under the pseudonym Michael Angelo Titmarsh, Thackeray lampooned the pompous Englishmen and importunate Arabs he encountered on his voyage.

There they lay, rosy and solemn in the distance, — those old, majestical, mystical, familiar edifices. Several of us [on board ship] tried to be impressed; but breakfast supervening, a rush was made at the coffee and cold pies, and the sentiment of awe was lost in the scramble for victuals.

Are we so blasés of the world that the greatest marvels in it do not succeed in moving us? Have society, Pall Mall clubs, and a habit of sneering, so withered up our organs of veneration that we can admire no more? My sensation with regard to the pyramids was, that I had seen them before: then came a feeling of shame that the view of them should awaken no respect. Then I wanted (naturally) to see whether my neighbors were any more enthusiastic than myself — Trinity College, Oxford, was busy with the cold ham: Downing Street was particularly attentive to a bunch of grapes: Fig Tree Court behaved with decent propriety; he is in good practice, and of a conservative turn of mind, which leads him to respect from principle *les faits accomplis;* perhaps he remembered that one of them was as big as Lincoln's Inn Fields. But, the truth is, nobody was seriously moved. . . . And why should they, because of an exaggeration of bricks ever so enormous? I confess, for my part, that the pyramids are very big. . . .

. . . Shelley's two sonnets are the best views that I know of the Pyramids — better than the reality; for a man may lay down the book, and in quiet fancy conjure up a picture out of these magnificent words, which shan't be disturbed by any pettinesses or mean realities, — such as the swarms of howling beggars, who jostle you about the actual place, and scream in your ears incessantly, and hang on your skirts, and bawl for money. . . .

. . . There they [the Pyramids] rose up enormous under our eyes, and the most absurd, trivial things were going on under their shadow. The sublime had disappeared, vast as they were. Do you remember how Gulliver lost his awe of the tremendous Brobdingnag ladies? Every traveller must go through all sorts of chaffering, and bargaining, and paltry experiences, at this spot. You look up the tremendous steps, with a score of savage ruffians bellowing round you; you hear faint cheers and cries high up, and catch sight of little reptiles crawling upwards: or, having achieved the summit, they come hopping and bouncing down again from degree to degree — the cheers and cries swell louder and more disagreeable; presently the little jumping thing, no bigger than an insect a moment ago, bounces down upon you expanded into a panting major of Bengal cavalry. He drives off the Arabs with an oath, — wipes his red, shining face, with his yellow handkerchief, drops puffing on the sand in a shady corner, where cold fowl and hard eggs are awaiting him, and the next minute you see his nose plunged in a foaming beaker of brandy and soda-water. He can say now and for ever, he has been up the Pyramid. There is nothing sublime in it. You cast your eye once more up that staggering perspective of a zigzag line, which ends at the summit, and wish you were up there — and down again. Forwards! Up with you! It must be done. Six Arabs are behind you, who wo'n't let you escape if you would.

The importunity of these ruffians is a ludicrous annoyance to which a traveller must submit. For two miles before you reach the Pyramids, they seize on you, and never cease howling. Five or six of them pounce upon one victim, and never leave him until they have carried him up and down. Sometimes they conspire to run a man up the huge stair, and bring him, half-killed and fainting, to the top. Always a couple of brutes insist upon impelling you sternwards; from whom the only means to release yourself is to kick out vigorously and unmercifully, when the Arabs will possibly retreat. The ascent is not the least romantic, or difficult, or sublime: you walk up a great broken staircase, of which some of the steps are four feet high. It's not hard, only a little high. You see no better view from the top than you beheld from the bottom; only a little more river, and sand, and rice field. You jump down the big steps at your leisure; but your meditations you must keep for after times, — the cursed shrieking of the Arabs prevents all thought or leisure.

— And this is all you have to tell about the Pyramids? O! for shame! Not a compliment to their age and size? Not a big phrase, — not a rapture? Do you mean to say that you had no feeling of respect and awe? Try, man, and build up a monument of words as lofty as they are. . . .

— No: be that work for great geniuses, great painters, great poets! This quill was never made to take such flights; it comes of the wing of an humble domestic bird, who walks a common; who talks a great deal (and hisses sometimes); who can't fly far or high, and drops always very quickly; and whose unromantic end is, to be laid on a Michaelmas or Christmas table, and there to be discussed for half an hour — let us hope, with some relish.

WILLIAM M. THACKERAY
Notes of a Journey from Cornhill to Grand Cairo, 1846

Upon retiring from the American presidency following an unusually scandal-racked administration, Ulysses S. Grant embarked on a worldwide tour. Accompanied by the former United States Consul General at Cairo, Elbert E. Farman, the general and his wife admired the pyramids at Giza — and, as Farman records, they discovered that the ex-president's fame had preceded him.

At the special request of the General [Grant] I invited General and Mrs. Stone to accompany us on this excursion. We passed through the city by the Ezbekîyeh gardens and the principal hotels and thence to the great Nile bridge. In crossing, we met a continuous line of camels and donkeys accompanied by fellâhîn, turbaned men, veiled women and squalid children. . . . The bridge, in the early morning hours, with the curious throng of natives and animals passing over it, is an interesting study to the student of oriental life. . . .

We moved at a rapid pace and were soon near the pyramids which had been in full view since we left the immediate vicinity of the river. They did not appear large to the General as we approached them. The first view was a little disappointing, like that of Niagara Falls. On our arrival we found a number of Americans awaiting General Grant and the photographer did not fail to put in an appearance and take the group with General and Mrs. Grant as the central figures and the great pyramid for a background.

A larger swarm of Arabs than usual, attracted from the villages near the road by the brilliancy of our equipage, had accompanied us for some distance, running beside and following after our vehicle clamoring for bakshîsh

[gratuities] and offering their services as guides in the ascent of the pyramids. On our arrival the number increased. But the gold lace uniform of Hassan, and his long, recurvated sword had a magic influence in keeping them at a respectful distance. When they learned that the chief of our party was no less a personage than the "King of America," as the Arabs always styled the ex-president, they moderated their noisy persistence and those who desired to make the ascent of the pyramid, selected their aids with little further annoyance. The General wisely decided not to make the ascent, but nearly all the others being younger, and ambitious of standing on the highest point, engaged their attendants and commenced what seemed an easy task. . . .

Sitting at the base of the pyramid while others were making the ascent, the General figured the amount of stone required in its construction, and made some estimates as to the cities that might be built from such an amount of material. His illustrious predecessor in Egypt, Napoleon the 1st, sitting near the same place, made similar computations. . . .

On the descent of those who had gone to the top, General and Mrs. Grant joined them in entering the pyramid. This is an exceedingly interesting, but in some respects, disagreeable task. The air is close and filled with fine dust and occasionally a bat, disturbed and blinded by the light of the candles and torches, comes whizzing by or strikes saucily against you. But there is no danger nor is there any place requiring any strain on the muscles as in the ascent likely to produce temporary lameness. The physical exertion is less than half that required to reach the top of the pyramid. . . .

We soon reached the open air and were glad to partake of the lunch that had been prepared and served in the Khedivial Kiosk, opened for the occasion. We then made the circuit of the plateau of the pyramids which covers nearly a square mile. Mrs. Grant rode a fine donkey; the others were on foot. We visited the second and third pyramid, a few of the numerous tombs belonging to the same period and containing some of the finest specimens of hieroglyphic writing that have come to us, the Sphinx, and others of the numerous and exceedingly interesting monuments of this ancient necropolis.

The sun was already approaching the horizon of the Libyan desert and the pyramids were casting long shadows over the bluish-green fields of the valley, admonishing us that we must leave this most hallowed place, consecrated at the very dawn of civilization. . . .

The Arabs, who had served us, were well paid and satisfied, but that did not prevent a great number who had remained unemployed among whom were many boys and girls, from following us a long distance, crying for bakshîsh. All these people have, from their earliest childhood, attended visitors to the pyramids and know a few words of most European languages. One bright eyed little fellow, who had shown his agility by keeping alongside of us, on being admonished to return, answered, "The others are contented," meaning those who had been paid; "I want to be contented too; everybody wants to be contented." He evidently thought that the "King of America," that land of fabulous riches, could easily "content" them all. A few coins were thrown out and there was a pell-mell scramble and the last words we heard were those of the boy, who had undoubtedly obtained his share, crying in a loud voice, "Everybody contented, everybody contented."

ELBERT E. FARMAN
Along the Nile with General Grant, 1904

General Summary, *first published in 1886 when Rudyard Kipling was only twenty-one, expresses the famed English author's gently jaundiced view of the nature of man — unchanged since the time of the pyramid builders more than three thousand years ago.*

We are very slightly changed
From the semi-apes who ranged
   India's prehistoric clay;
Whoso drew the longest bow,
Ran his brother down, you know,
   As we run men down to-day.

"Dowb," the first of all his race,
Met the Mammoth face to face
   On the lake or in the cave,
Stole the steadiest canoe,
Ate the quarry others slew,
   Died — and took the finest grave.

When they scratched the reindeer-bone,
Someone made the sketch his own,
   Filched it from the artist — then,
Even in those early days,
Won a simple Viceroy's praise
   Through the toil of other men.

Ere they hewed the Sphinx's visage,
Favoritism governed kissage,
Even as it does in this age.

Who shall doubt the secret hid
Under Cheops' pyramid
Was that the contractor did
   Cheops out of several millions?
Or that Joseph's sudden rise
To Comptroller of Supplies
Was a fraud of monstrous size
   On King Pharaoh's swart Civilians?

Thus, the artless songs I sing
Do not deal with anything
   New or never said before.
As it was in the beginning,
Is to-day official sinning,
   And shall be for evermore!

        RUDYARD KIPLING
        General Summary, 1886

In George Bernard Shaw's play Caesar *and* Cleopatra, *the ruthless and sensual queen is transformed into a childish and guileless heroine. In this scene from Act I, the last Ptolemaic ruler of Egypt has a fateful rendezvous in the shadow of what first appears to be the great Sphinx.*

The same darkness into which the temple of Ra and the Syrian palace vanished. The same silence. Suspense. Then the blackness and stillness break softly into silver mist and strange airs as the windswept harp of Memnon plays at the dawning of the moon. It rises full over the desert; and a vast horizon comes into relief, broken by a huge shape which soon reveals itself in the spreading radiance as a Sphinx pedestalled on the sands. The light still clears, until the upraised eyes of the image are distinguished looking straight forward and upward in infinite fearless vigil, and a mass of color between its great paws defines itself as a heap of red poppies on which a girl lies motionless, her silken vest heaving gently and regularly with the breathing of a dreamless sleeper, and her braided hair glittering in a shaft of moonlight like a bird's wing.

Suddenly there comes from afar a vaguely fearful sound (it might be the bellow of a Minotaur softened by great distance) and Memnon's music stops. Silence: then a few faint high-ringing trumpet notes. Then silence again. Then a man comes from the south with stealing steps, ravished by the mystery of the night, all wonder, and halts, lost in contemplation, opposite the left flank of the Sphinx, whose bosom, with its burden, is hidden from him by its massive shoulder.

THE MAN   Hail, Sphinx: salutation from Julius Caesar! I have wandered in many lands, seeking the lost regions from which my birth into this world exiled me, and the company of creatures such as I myself. I have found flocks and pastures, men and cities, but no other Caesar, no air native to me, no man kindred to me, none who can do my day's deed, and think my night's thought. In the little world yonder, Sphinx, my place is as high as yours in this great desert; only I wander, and you sit still; I conquer, and you endure; I work and wonder, you watch and wait; I look up and am dazzled, look down and am darkened, look round and am puzzled, whilst your eyes never turn from looking out — out of the world — to the lost region — the home from which we have strayed. Sphinx, you and I, strangers to the race of men, are no strangers to one another: have I not been conscious of you and of this place since I was born? Rome is a madman's dream: this is my Reality. These starry lamps of yours I have seen from afar in Gaul, in Britain, in Spain, in Thessaly, signalling great secrets to some eternal sentinel below, whose post I never could find. And here at last is their sentinel — an image of the constant and immortal part of my life, silent, full of thoughts, alone in the silver desert. Sphinx, Sphinx: I have climbed mountains at night to hear in the distance the stealthy footfall of the winds that chase your sands in forbidden play — our invisible children, O Sphinx, laughing in whispers. My way hither was the way of destiny; for I am he of whose genius you are the symbol: part brute, part woman, and part god — nothing of man in me at all. Have I read your riddle, Sphinx?

THE GIRL (*who has wakened, and peeped cautiously from her nest to see who is speaking*)   Old gentleman.

CAESAR (*starting violently, and clutching his sword*)   Immortal gods!

THE GIRL   Old gentleman: dont run away.

153

CAESAR (*stupefied*) "Old gentleman: dont run away"!!! This! to Julius Caesar!

THE GIRL (*urgently*) Old gentleman.

CAESAR Sphinx: you presume on your centuries. I am younger than you, though your voice is but a girl's voice as yet.

THE GIRL Climb up here, quickly; or the Romans will come and eat you.

CAESAR (*running forward past the Sphinx's shoulder, and seeing her*) A child at its breast! a divine child!

THE GIRL Come up quickly. You must get up at its side and creep round.

CAESAR (*amazed*) Who are you?

THE GIRL Cleopatra, Queen of Egypt.

CAESAR Queen of the Gypsies, you mean.

CLEOPATRA You must not be disrespectful to me, or the Sphinx will let the Romans eat you. Come up. It is quite cosy here.

CAESAR (*to himself*) What a dream! What a magnificent dream! Only let me not wake, and I will conquer ten continents to pay for dreaming it out to the end. (*He climbs to the Sphinx's flank, and presently reappears to her on the pedestal, stepping round its right shoulder*).

CLEOPATRA Take care. Thats right. Now sit down: you may have its other paw. (*She seats herself comfortably on its left paw*). It is very powerful and will protect us; but (*shivering, and with plaintive loneliness*) it would not take any notice of me or keep me company. I am glad you have come: I was very lonely. Did you happen to see a white cat anywhere?

CAESAR (*sitting slowly down on the right paw in extreme wonderment*) Have you lost one?

CLEOPATRA Yes: the sacred white cat: is it not dreadful? I brought him here to sacrifice him to the Sphinx; but when we got a little way from the city a black cat called him, and he jumped out of my arms and ran away to it. Do you think that the black cat can have been my great-great-great-grandmother?

CAESAR (*staring at her*) Your great-great-great-grandmother! Well, why not? Nothing would surprise me on this night of nights.

CLEOPATRA I think it must have been. My great-grandmother's great-grandmother was a black kitten of the sacred white cat; and the river Nile made her his seventh wife. That is why my hair is so wavy. And I always want to be let do as I like, no matter whether it is the will of the gods or not: that is because my blood is made with Nile water.

CAESAR What are you doing here at this time of night? Do you live here?

CLEOPATRA Of course not: I am the Queen; and I shall live in the palace at Alexandria when I have killed my brother, who drove me out of it. When I am old enough I shall do just what I like. I shall be able to poison the slaves and see them wriggle, and pretend to Ftatateeta that she is going to be put into the fiery furnace.

CAESAR ·Hm! Meanwhile why are you not at home and in bed?

CLEOPATRA Because the Romans are coming to eat us all. You are not at home and in bed either.

CAESAR (*with conviction*) Yes I am. I live in a tent; and I am now in that tent, fast asleep and dreaming. Do you suppose that I believe you are real, you impossible little dream witch?

CLEOPATRA (*giggling and leaning trustfully towards him*) You are a funny old gentleman. I like you.

CAESAR   Ah, that spoils the dream. Why dont you dream that I am young?

CLEOPATRA   I wish you were; only I think I should be more afraid of you. I like men, especially young men with round strong arms; but I am afraid of them. You are old and rather thin and stringy; but you have a nice voice; and I like to have somebody to talk to, though I think you are a little mad. It is the moon that makes you talk to yourself in that silly way.

CAESAR   What! you heard that, did you? I was saying my prayers to the great Sphinx.

CLEOPATRA   But this isnt the great Sphinx.

CAESAR (*much disappointed, looking up at the statue*)   What!

CLEOPATRA   This is only a dear little kitten of a Sphinx. Why, the great Sphinx is so big that it has a temple between its paws. This is my pet Sphinx. Tell me: do you think the Romans have any sorcerers who could take us away from the Sphinx by magic?

CAESAR   Why? Are you afraid of the Romans?

CLEOPATRA (*very seriously*)   Oh, they would eat us if they caught us. They are barbarians. Their chief is called Julius Caesar. His father was a tiger and his mother a burning mountain; and his nose is like an elephant's trunk. (*Caesar involuntarily rubs his nose*). They all have long noses, and ivory tusks, and little tails, and seven arms with a hundred arrows in each; and they live on human flesh.

CAESAR   Would you like me to shew you a real Roman?

CLEOPATRA (*terrified*)   No. You are frightening me.

CAESAR   No matter: this is only a dream —

CLEOPATRA (*excitedly*)   It is not a dream: it is not a dream. See, see. (*She plucks a pin from her hair and jabs it repeatedly into his arm*).

CAESAR   Ffff — Stop. (*Wrathfully*) How dare you?

CLEOPATRA (*abashed*)   You said you were dreaming. (*Whimpering*) I only wanted to shew you —

CAESAR (*gently*)   Come, come: dont cry. A queen mustnt cry. (*He rubs his arm, wondering at the reality of the smart*). Am I awake? (*He strikes his hand against the Sphinx to test its solidity. It feels so real that he begins to be alarmed, and says perplexedly*) Yes, I — (*quite panicstricken*) no: impossible: madness, madness! (*Desperately*) Back to camp — to camp. (*He rises to spring down from the pedestal*).

CLEOPATRA (*flinging her arms in terror round him*)   No: you shant leave me. No, no, no: dont go. I'm afraid — afraid of the Romans.

CAESAR (*as the conviction that he is really awake forces itself on him*)   Cleopatra: can you see my face well?

CLEOPATRA   Yes. It is so white in the moonlight.

CAESAR   Are you sure it is the moonlight that makes me look whiter than an Egyptian? (*Grimly*) Do you notice that I have a rather long nose?

CLEOPATRA (*recoiling, paralysed by a terrible suspicion*)   Oh!

CAESAR   It is a Roman nose, Cleopatra.

CLEOPATRA   Ah! (*With a piercing scream she springs up; darts round the left shoulder of the Sphinx; scrambles down to the sand; and falls on her knees in frantic supplication, shrieking*) Bite him in two, Sphinx: bite him in two. I meant to sacrifice the white cat — I did indeed — I (*Caesar, who has slipped down from the pedestal, touches her on the shoulder*) — Ah! (*She buries her head in her arms*).

CAESAR   Cleopatra: shall I teach you a way to prevent Caesar from eating you?

CLEOPATRA (*clinging to him piteously*) Oh do, do, do. I will steal Ftatateeta's jewels and give them to you. I will make the river Nile water your lands twice a year.

CAESAR Peace, peace, my child. Your gods are afraid of the Romans: you see the Sphinx dare not bite me, nor prevent me carrying you off to Julius Caesar.

CLEOPATRA (*in pleading murmurings*) You wont, you wont. You said you wouldnt.

CAESAR Caesar never eats women.

CLEOPATRA (*springing up full of hope*) What!

CAESAR (*impressively*) But he eats girls (*she relapses*) and cats. Now you are a silly little girl; and you are descended from the black kitten. You are both a girl and a cat.

CLEOPATRA (*trembling*) And will he eat me?

CAESAR Yes; unless you make him believe that you are a woman.

CLEOPATRA Oh, you must get a sorcerer to make a woman of me. Are you a sorcerer?

CAESAR Perhaps. But it will take a long time; and this very night you must stand face to face with Caesar in the palace of your fathers.

CLEOPATRA No, no. I darent.

CAESAR Whatever dread may be in your soul — however terrible Caesar may be to you — you must confront him as a brave woman and a great queen; and you must feel no fear. If your hand shakes: if your voice quavers; then — night and death! (*She moans*). But if he thinks you worthy to rule, he will set you on the throne by his side and make you the real ruler of Egypt.

GEORGE BERNARD SHAW
Caesar and Cleopatra, 1900

THE ENDURING MYSTERY

The origin of the pyramids has been a source of fascination for centuries. In 1646 John Greaves, a professor of astronomy at Oxford, recorded — with grave misgivings about its accuracy — the most prominent Arabic explanation.

The Arabian writers, especially such as have purposely treated of the wonders of Egypt have given us a more full description [of the Pyramids]: but that hath been mixed with so many inventions of their owne, that the truth hath been darkned, and almost extinguished by them. I shall put downe that which is confessed by them, to be the most probable relation, as is reported by Ibn Abd Alhokm, whose words out of the Arabick are these.

The greatest part of Chronologers agree, that he which built the Pyramids was Saurid Ibn Salhouk, King of Egypt, who lived three hundred years before the flood. The occasion of this was because he saw in his sleep, that the whole earth was turned over, with the inhabitants of it, the men lying upon their faces, and the stars falling downe and striking one another, with a terrible noise, and being troubled with this, he concealed it. Then after he saw the fixt stars falling to the earth, in the similitude of white fowle, and they snatched up men, and carried them between two great mountaines, and these mountaines closed upon them, and the shining stars were made darke. And he awaked with great feare, and assembled the chief Priests of all the Provinces of Egypt, an hundred and thirty priests, the chief of them was called Aclimun. He related the whole matter to them, and they took the alti-

156

tude of the stars, and made their prognostication, and they foretold of a deluge. The king said will it come to our country? They answered yea, and will destroy it. And there remained a certain number of years to come, and he commanded in the mean space to build the Pyramids, and that a vault (or cisterne) should be made, into which the river Nilus should enter, from whence it should runne into the countries of the West, and into the land Al-Said.

And he filled them [the Pyramids] with talismans, and with strange things, and with riches, and treasures, and the like. He engraved in them all things that were told him by wise men, as also all profound sciences, the names of alakakirs, the uses, and hurts of them. The science of Astrology, and of Arithmeticke, and of Geometry, and of Physicke. All this may be interpreted by him that knowes their characters, and language. After he had given orders for this building, they cut out vast columnes, and wonderfull stones. They fetched massy stones from the Ethiopians, and made with these the foundations of the three Pyramids, fastening them together with lead, and iron. They built the gates of them 40 cubits under ground, and they made the height of the Pyramids 100 royall cubits, which are 500 of ours in these times. He also made each side of them an hundred royall cubits. The beginning of this building was in a fortunate horoscope. After that he had finished it, he covered it with coloured Satten [marble], from the top to the bottome and he appointed a solemne festivall, at which were present all the inhabitants of his Kingdome. Then he built in the Westerne Pyramid thirty treasuries, filled with store of riches, and utensils, and with signatures made of precious stones, and with instruments of iron, and vessels of earth, and with a mes which rusts not, and with glasse which might be bended, and yet not broken, and with strange spells, and with severall kinds of akakirs, single, and double, and with deadly poisons, and with other things besides. He made also in the East Pyramid, divers celestiall spheres, and stars, and what they severally operate, in their aspects; and the perfumes which are to be used to them and the books which treat of these matters.

He put also in the coloured Pyramid [the third], the commentaries of the Priests, in chests of black marble, and with every Priest a booke, in which were the wonders of his profession, and of his actions, and of his nature, and what was done in his time, and what is, and what shall be, from the beginning of time, to the end of it. He placed in every Pyramid a Treasurer: the treasurer of the westerly Pyramid was a statue of marble stone standing upright with a lance, and upon his head a Serpent wreathed. He that came neare it, and stood still, the Serpent bit him of one side, and wreathed round his throat, and killed him, and then returned to his place. He made the treasurer of the East Pyramid an idoll of black Agate, his eyes open, and shining, sitting upon a throne with a lance; when any lookt upon him, he heard of one side of him a voice, which took away his sense, so that he fell prostrate upon his face, and ceased not till he died. He made the treasurer of the Coloured Pyramid a statue of stone, called Albut, sitting. He which looked towards it was drawn by the statue, till he stucke to it, and could not be separated from it, till such time as he died.

Thus farre the Arabians: which traditions of theirs are little better than a romance.

JOHN GREAVES
Pyramidographia, 1646

In the nineteenth century another astronomer applied himself to the problem of the derivation of the pyramids. Employing a mixture of scientific mumbo jumbo and biblical mythology, Charles Piazzi Smyth devised a fantastically complex numerological system.

The late Mr. John Taylor of London, in a book published in A.D. 1859, and entitled "The Great Pyramid; why was it built? and who built it?" . . . successfully deduced sound and Christian reasons for believing that the director of the building [of the Great Pyramid], and perhaps his immediate assistants who controlled the myriads of *native* builders at the Great Pyramid, were by no means Egyptians, but strangers of the *chosen* race. . . .

. . . after disobeying the world's long-formed public opinion of too passively obedient accord with profane Egyptian tradition . . . [Mr. Taylor] announced that he had discovered in some of the arrangements and measures of the Great Pyramid — when duly corrected for injuries and dilapidations of intervening time — certain scientific results, which speak of neither Egyptian nor Babylonian, and much less of Greek or Roman learning, but of something much more than, as well as quite different from, any ordinary human ways of those several contemporary times.

. . . the actual facts of the Great Pyramid, in the shape of builded proofs of an exact numerical knowledge of the grander cosmical phenomena of both earth and heavens — not only rise above, and far above, the extremely limited and almost infantine knowledge of science humanly attained to by any of the Gentile nations of 4000, 3000, 2000, nay only 300 years ago; but they are also, in whatever of the great physical secrets of nature they chiefly apply to, essentially above the best knowledge of philosophers in our own time as well. . . .

. . . in the truly primeval day when men were few on the earth, . . . the Great Pyramid was built, finished, sealed up, and left as we see it now, modern dilapidations only excepted, in the midst of an unbelieving world, to guard its own secret through the ages, and serve at last its intended purpose, whatever that was to be, in the latter days of mankind. . . .

. . . Mr. Taylor . . . ventured the suggestion, that the author of the Great Pyramid's design employed both decimal and quinary arithmetic; and did actually use, as his smaller unit of linear measure, the one-fifth part of a one-fifth of his general standard of the Great Pyramid. . . .

Now the small *unit* of measure so obtained, measures over the *standard's* length 25 even, where British inches measure 25.025; and one Great Pyramid unit, or inch, equals 1.001 British inch; or is larger than a British inch, but only by so small a quantity as half a hair's breadth. An apparently unimportant feature, and yet it is by the Pyramid inch being just so much larger and no more, that it becomes evenly, and Pyramidally *earth-commensurable;* so that *five* hundred millions of *them,* and not of British inches, measure the length of the earth's axis of rotation evenly and with exactitude, and constitute a Pyramid number. . . .

As in squaring the circle, so in measuring the distance of the earth's heating sun, both learned and unlearned in the schools of men have been working at the question for 2300 years and are still for ever employing themselves upon it. . . . Yet even the best of modern nations, are far from having arrived at even tolerable exactness. Nevertheless *there* of old, before the beginning of any human science, is the numerical expression for that cos-

mical, sun-distance quantity, to almost any refinement, nailed to the mast of the Great Pyramid from the earliest ages; for it is its mast or vertical height, multiplied by its own factor, the ninth power of ten, which is the length all modern men are seeking, and struggling after; in one attempt overshooting, in another falling below, and so going on hundreds of times without ever hitting the mark exactly. And there also in the base-side length from socket to socket of the building, *when measured by the sacred cubit appointed by God,* (viz. the one-ten-millionth of the terrestrial semi-axis of rotation), is the number of turns and parts of a turn made by the earth on its axis, as it revolves in the equivalent circle of that gigantic mean radial distance of the sun.

CHARLES PIAZZI SMYTH
Our Inheritance in the Great Pyramid, 1864

Unless one is a fanciful dreamer such as Smyth, archaeology is a serious, painstaking profession. Richard Lepsius, leader of the 1843 German expedition to Egypt that uncovered the remains of thirty Old Kingdom tombs, did manage to add a note of levity to his task.

Still here! in full activity since the 9th of November, and perhaps to continue so for some weeks of the new year! How could I have anticipated from the accounts of previous travellers, what a harvest we were to reap here, — here, on the oldest stage of the chronologically definable history of mankind. It is remarkable how little this most frequented place of all Egypt has been examined hitherto. But I will not quarrel with our predecessors, since we inherit the fruits of their inactivity. I have been obliged the rather to restrain our curiosity to see more of this wonder-land, as we may have solved the problem of this place. . . .

I employ forty to sixty people every day in excavations and similar labours. Also before the great Sphinx I have had excavations made to bring to light the temple between its paws, and to lay open the colossal stele formed of one block of granite, eleven feet high and seven feet broad, serving as a back wall to the temple, and covered to about its own height with sand. . . .

. . . On the evening of the first Christmas holiday, I surprised my companions by a large bonfire, which I had lighted at the top of the greatest pyramid. The flame shown magnificently upon the two other pyramids, as well as on the Necropolis, and threw its light far over the dale to Cairo. That was a Christmas pyramid! I had only confided the secret to Abeken, who had arrived, with his ever merry humour and his animated and instructive conversation, upon the 10th of December. With his assistance I prepared something for the following night, in the Royal Chamber of the Great Pyramid. We planted a young palm-tree in the sarcophagus of the ancient king, and adorned it with lights and little presents that I had sent for from the city for us children of the wilderness. . . . On New Year's eve, at midnight, there arose mighty flames from the heights of the three great pyramids, and announced, far and wide in the regions of Islam, at their feet, the change of the Christian year.

RICHARD LEPSIUS
Discoveries in Egypt, Ethiopia, and the Peninsula of Sinai, 1843

At the age of seventy-seven, Flinders Petrie surveyed a lifetime of excavation and discovery in Egypt. In this description of his surveying techniques at Giza in 1880, the renowned Egyptologist sums up the credo of a dedicated archaeologist.

It was often most convenient to strip entirely for work, owing to the heat and absence of any current of air, in the interior [of the Great Pyramid]. For outside work in the hot weather, vest and pants were suitable, and if pink they kept the tourist at bay, as the creature seemed to him too queer for inspection. After rigging up the rock-tomb with shelves, and re-making the old shutters and door, which had been left by Dixon, I found the place comfortable. The petroleum stove by the door cooked my meals, which I prepared at any time required by the irregular hours of work.

When the big theodolite was out, it was needful to finish a stretch of observing within the day, which left only time for a morning and evening feed, and I always reduced the observations every night. On days when work lay inside the pyramid, the morning was spent in writing up observations, and the hours of interior measurement ran from about five till midnight. A negro slave of Aly, and a little nephew of his, used to sleep in the next tomb, as night guard. . . .

My position was expressed in a letter to Spurrell, some months before I went out. "So much has been lost through not allowing for the possibility of a higher value existing — whether in accuracy of construction, or in care and regularity of dimensions — or by digging barrows over by the spadeful anyhow — that a radical change is required in the way of doing all such things, and I do not wish to rest until whatever care may have been bestowed on ancient work is brought to light. This is almost universally misunderstood, and I am accustomed to be accused of trying to find something that never existed, though a gold digger is not thought foolish for washing a pan of earth on the thousandth of a chance of finding a nugget. He does not expect it, but takes the only means of finding it, if it is there. So do I."

FLINDERS PETRIE
Seventy Years in Archaeology, 1932

REFERENCE

Chronology of Egyptian History

Five thousand years have elapsed since the unification of Egypt. Those millennia have been punctuated by plagues and famines, usurpations and assassinations, military expeditions and foreign incursions — civil clashes and international crises that have obscured or erased many key dates in ancient Egyptian history. As a result, chronologies of the thirty dynasties of ancient Egypt are a matter of scholarly conjecture, and each differs slightly from all others. The table below draws heavily upon one of the most reliable of contemporary chronologies, the revised edition of *The Cambridge Ancient History*.

ARCHAIC PERIOD

FIRST DYNASTY *c.* 3100–2890 B.C.

Narmer unifies Upper and Lower Egypt and establishes his capital at Memphis

SECOND DYNASTY *c.* 2890–2686 B.C.

Period of strife ended by Khasekhemwy

OLD KINGDOM

THIRD DYNASTY *c.* 2686–2613 B.C.

Zoser builds the Step Pyramid at Sakkara

FOURTH DYNASTY *c.* 2613–2494 B.C.

Snofru builds the Bent Pyramid and the first true pyramid at Dahshur

Great Pyramid constructed by Cheops at Giza

Chephren erects the second pyramid and the Sphinx

Third pyramid built by Mycerinus

FIFTH DYNASTY *c.* 2494–2345 B.C.

Earliest known text of the *Book of the Dead* inscribed within King Unas's pyramid at Sakkara

SIXTH DYNASTY *c.* 2345–2181 B.C.

Period of growing chaos follows reign of Pepi II

FIRST INTERMEDIATE PERIOD

SEVENTH—TENTH DYNASTIES *c.* 2181–2040 B.C.

Breakdown of central authority

MIDDLE KINGDOM

ELEVENTH DYNASTY *c.* 2133–1991 B.C.

Mentuhotep II reunifies Upper and Lower Egypt, establishes capital at Thebes, and builds mortuary temple at Deir el-Bahri

TWELFTH DYNASTY *c.* 1991–1786 B.C.

Amenhemet I moves court near Memphis; god Amen gains prominence; period of high cultural advancement

SECOND INTERMEDIATE PERIOD

THIRTEENTH—SEVENTEENTH DYNASTIES *c.* 1786–1567 B.C.

Period of internal strife among warring rulers

NEW KINGDOM

EIGHTEENTH DYNASTY 1567–1320 B.C.

Ahmose ousts Hyksos from Lower Egypt and reunites country

Amenhotep I strengthens Egyptian control over Nubia

Tuthmosis I extends national boundaries beyond Fourth Cataract

Queen Hashepsowe builds mortuary temple at Deir el-Bahri

Tuthmosis III extends empire from Syria to the Sudan; defeats prince of Kadesh in the battle of Megiddo

Tuthmosis IV clears sand from Sphinx

Amenhotep IV changes name to Akhenaten and attempts to institute monotheistic worship of the sun-disk Aten

Tutankhamen reverses Akhenaten's religious revolution

Horemheb institutes administrative reforms

NINETEENTH DYNASTY 1320–1200 B.C.

Seti I begins work on Hypostyle Hall

Ramesses II wages war against the Hittites, completes Hypostyle Hall at temple of Amen-Re at Karnak, and builds vast temples at Thebes and Abu Simbel

TWENTIETH DYNASTY 1200–1085 B.C.

Ramesses III repulses invasion of the Sea Peoples

Reign of Ramesses XI ends the New Kingdom

THIRD INTERMEDIATE PERIOD

TWENTY-FIRST—TWENTY-FOURTH DYNASTIES 1085–710 B.C.

Period of overlapping rulers; invasion by Assyrians

LATE DYNASTIC PERIOD

TWENTY-FIFTH DYNASTY 736–656 B.C.

Egypt ruled by Kushite pharaohs

TWENTY-SIXTH DYNASTY 664–525 B.C.

Psammetichos I wins independence from Assyria and establishes the Saite dynasty

TWENTY-SEVENTH DYNASTY 525–404 B.C.

Conquest by the Great King Cambyses establishes first Persian domination of Egypt

TWENTY-EIGHTH—THIRTIETH DYNASTIES 404–341 B.C.

Last rulers of an independent Egypt

341–333 B.C.	Second Persian domination of Egypt
332	Alexander the Great conquers country and founds city of Alexandria
304	One of Alexander's generals establishes the Ptolemaic dynasty
c. 280	Egyptian priest Manetho groups ancient pharaohs into dynastic divisions
47–30	Reign of Cleopatra VII, last Ptolemaic ruler
31	Octavian defeats Antony and Cleopatra at the battle of Actium
30	Egypt becomes a province of Rome
324–640 A.D.	Coptic and Byzantine period
451	Egyptian Christians espouse Monophysite heresy
641	Moslems under Amr conquer Egypt
661–750	Egypt under rule of the Omayyads
750	Abbasid Caliphate established
813–833	Caliph Mamun hacks opening in the Great Pyramid in search of treasure
969	Fatimids conquer Egypt and establish their capital at Cairo
1171	Saladin overthrows Fatimids and founds Ayyubid dynasty
1193–98	Saladin's son attempts to demolish the third pyramid at Giza
1250	Mamelukes become ruling sultans
1517	Ottoman Turks conquer Egypt
1798–99	Bonaparte's expedition to Egypt; finding of the Rosetta Stone
1801	French forces withdraw from Egypt
1811	Muhammad Ali, founder of modern Egypt, massacres Mamelukes in Cairo
1822	Rosetta Stone deciphered by Champollion
1839–41	War with Ottoman sultan; Muhammad Ali secures hereditary tenure over Egypt
1849	Death of Muhammad Ali
1859	Work begun on Suez Canal
1869	Suez Canal officially opened
1875	Khedive Ismail sells his shares in Suez Canal Company to the British government
1879	Acting under Anglo-French pressure, sultan deposes Ismail
1880	Flinders Petrie initiates scientific excavation of ancient sites
1882	British army occupies Egypt
1883	Evelyn Baring appointed consul-general
1884	Egypt evacuates and abandons the Sudan
1885	Khartoum besieged
1888	Suez Canal Convention, signed by major powers, declares canal open to shipping of all nations
1896–98	Reconquest of the Sudan
1906	Turkey renounces claim to Sinai Peninsula
1907	First Nationalist Party organized
1911	Lord Kitchener named consul-general
1914	Egypt proclaimed a British protectorate
1919	Egyptian nationalist insurrection
1922	Termination of British protectorate; Fuad I becomes king of independent Egypt
1922	Howard Carter discovers the tomb of the boy-king Tutankhamen
1923	Promulgation of new constitution
1925–30	Nationalist party gains strength
1936	Farouk becomes king
1940	Italian army invades Egypt
1945	Arab League formed
1948	U.N. truce ends Arab-Israeli war
1952	Military coup overthrows King Farouk
1954	Colonel Gamal Abdel Nasser named premier of Egypt
1956	Nasser elected president, nationalizes Suez Canal; Israeli, Anglo-French forces invade, withdraw under U.N. supervision
1958	Egypt and Syria form United Arab Republic
1960	Construction of Aswan High Dam begun
1961	Syria withdraws from the U.A.R.
1964	First stage of Aswan High Dam completed
1966–68	Temples at Abu Simbel moved to high ground above Lake Nasser
1967	Six-Day War with Israel
1970	Death of Nasser
1971	Inauguration of Aswan High Dam

Guide to Egyptian Monuments

For thousands of years, the powerful pharaohs of Egypt built monumental structures of stone. The three pyramids at Giza are undoubtedly the most famous of these monuments — in the popular imagination, they have become synonymous with Egypt itself. Viewed from the perspective of Egyptian tomb architecture, however, the pyramids are only one stage in a long process of development and experimentation.

At Sakkara, twelve miles south of the Giza plateau, rises the forerunner of the pyramids, the Step Pyramid of Zoser. Its architect was Imhotep, an innovative genius who was the first Egyptian to reject brick and build entirely in stone.

The massive limestone tomb that Imhotep constructed to house the body of Zoser, founder of the Third Dynasty, is a remarkable departure from tradition. Previously, pharaohs had been buried in *mastabas*—oblong-shaped structures with sloping brick walls. Imhotep built a 26-foot-high *mastaba* composed of small blocks of stone laid out like bricks on a square ground plan. On top of this nucleus he then set five successively smaller *mastabas,* one on top of another. The final structure, over two hundred feet high, resembles a giant flight of stairs.

Zoser's successors in the Third Dynasty erected variants of his Step Pyramid, but none were as impressive in size or design. At the beginning of the Fourth Dynasty the first true pyramid — with sides sloping in an unbroken line to a point at the summit — was built by the pharaoh Snofru at Dahshur, just south of Sakkara. Snofru's second monument, the well-preserved Bent Pyramid, takes its name from its unusual shape:

at a point somewhat above half its height the angle of inclination decreases sharply. One theory holds that the pyramid may have been rushed to completion — and therefore the angle was changed to reduce the final height.

Snofru's son and successor was Cheops, who built the Great Pyramid — apogee of the art of pyramid building. Yet even this triumphant structure failed to accomplish its purpose: despite the elaborate precautions taken by Cheops and later pharaohs, tomb thieves managed to penetrate and rob these highly conspicuous structures of the sacred corpse and the treasure they were to guard through eternity. Although tomb pyramids continued to be built in succeeding dynasties, they were ultimately superseded by vast temple complexes near which the body of the pharaoh was ever more carefully concealed.

All along the fertile banks of the Nile — from the Delta in Lower (northern) Egypt to Abu Simbel in Upper (southern) Egypt — the ruling monarchs guaranteed their immortality by constructing temples, mortuary complexes, tombs, and palaces. The greatest flowering of architectural opulence and beauty was centered around Thebes in Upper Egypt. Showy, grandiose, and overwhelming — even in ruins these monuments testify to the glory of Egyptian aesthetic imagination.

Thebes reached its greatest prominence during the Eighteenth and Nineteenth dynasties. Bounded by elaborate temple complexes on the north at modern Karnak and on the south at present-day Luxor, the east bank was the magnificent cultural and commercial quarter of the metropolis. On the west bank of

the Nile the pharaohs created an entire "city of the dead," consisting of elaborate funerary temples and the famous Valley of the Kings.

The first pharaoh to build on a monumental scale at Thebes was Mentuhotep II, founder of the Eleventh Dynasty. His temple on the west bank at Deir el-Bahri is set against the rocky Theban cliffs. Rising in three terraced stages topped by a pyramid, the tomb complex is approached by a porticoed courtyard.

Mentuhotep's relatively modest structure became the inspiration for one of the most beautiful buildings in Egypt — the mortuary temple of the controversial Eighteenth Dynasty female pharaoh, Hashepsowe. Her architect was the court favorite Senmut, who planned her lavish temple at Deir el-Bahri as an integrated unit, taking full advantage of the inherent drama of the site. The golden limestone temple seems to form part of the landscape: a series of colonnaded shrines mounts, on three long terraces linked by causeways, to sanctuaries, funerary chapels, and the hills beyond. Despite the depredations of her successor, Tuthmosis III, Hashepsowe's breathtaking monument remains substantially as it was when first built in the fifteenth century B.C.

Hashepsowe chose as the site of her tomb a remote spot beyond the eastern face of the cliffs. Her father, Tuthmosis I, had been the first to be buried in the secluded canyon of this Valley of the Kings. Other pharaohs followed their example, carving deep tunnels and narrow stairways into the rock in a vain attempt to outwit tomb thieves. By the end of the Twentieth Dynasty some sixty burial chambers had been hidden in the secret recesses of this underground necropolis. Only one — the treasure-filled tomb of a minor Eighteenth Dynasty pharaoh, Tutankhamen — has been found virtually intact.

Tuthmosis III devoted much of his architectural efforts to the temple of Amen-Re at Karnak. The original structure had been a small shrine dedicated to an obscure god. As the importance of Amen grew, so did his temple. Tuthmosis I and Hashepsowe laid out the basic features; Tuthmosis III enlarged it, adding a vast pavilion, carved obelisks, massive pylons, and sloping gateways. Succeeding pharaohs added to the temple until it finally became the largest religious structure in the world. A processional avenue of one thousand recumbent sphinxes linked the temple of Karnak to Luxor, two miles upriver.

Another Eighteenth Dynasty ruler, Amenhotep III, also built his mortuary temple at Karnak. All that remains of that temple, which was larger than that of any other Theban ruler, are two mutilated, seventy-foot-high seated effigies standing in isolated splendor in the fields. These majestic statues, known as the Colossi of Memnon, were each carved from a single block of sandstone.

Amenhotep III's heretical son Akhenaten built a new capital halfway between Luxor and Cairo, at Tell el-Amarna. His six-mile-long city on the Nile was dedicated to the sun disk Aten; only extensive excavated ruins mark the spot, for after Akhenaten's death the site was abandoned and the court returned to Thebes.

Egypt's most energetic builder was the Nineteenth Dynasty warrior-king Ramesses II. At Abydos, south of Tell el-Amarna, he dedicated a vast temple complex to Osiris. At Luxor he added to Amenhotep III's temple to Amen-Re a colonnaded court with six giant statues of himself. At Karnak, Ramesses II completed the largest structure in the temple complex, the Hypostyle Hall. Covering an area of 6,000 square yards, the hall consists of 134 richly decorated columns arranged in 16 rows. The tallest of these papyrus-shaped pillars is 79 feet high. The huge stone-slabbed roof has disappeared, leaving the columns exposed to the sky.

Ramesses II's mortuary temple on the west bank of Thebes, known as the Ramesseum, is a shattered ruin. Its major relic is a gray granite head that measures six feet from ear to ear, once part of a colossal statue of the pharaoh.

Two immense temples cut into the sandstone cliffs at Abu Simbel in Nubia are Ramesses II's most enduring monuments. On the façade of the larger temple, which faces the Nile, are four seated effigies of Ramesses, each over sixty-five feet high. In the interior of the temple are numerous chambers, statues, pillars, and a hypostyle hall cut deep into the rock. A few hundred feet to the north is the smaller temple, dedicated to his wife, Nefertari, and the goddess Hathor. Flanking the entrance are six statues of the king and his queen, each more than thirty feet high. Serene guardians of the Nile for fourteen centuries, both temples were threatened when the High Dam was built at Aswan in the 1960's. Cut out of the rock and meticulously reassembled atop the cliffs at Abu Simbel, Ramesses II's monuments may well endure for another fourteen centuries.

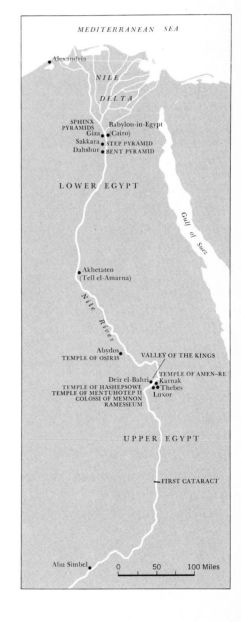

Seven Wonders of the Ancient World

Of the seven monuments listed by the Greeks in the second century B.C. as Wonders of the World, only one remains intact in the twentieth century. Ironically, this sole survivor — the pyramids at Giza in Egypt — is both the oldest and largest. Our scanty knowledge of the other six Wonders rests upon minute fragments, contemporary accounts, and artists' reconstructions.

The *Pyramids at Giza* were erected by three Old Kingdom pharaohs in the third millennium B.C. Long since robbed

of their treasure, these royal tombs continue to excite the imagination of tourist and scientist alike.

The pharaoh Cheops selected the most conspicuous spot on the desert plateau for his Great Pyramid. On a thirteen-acre site rises the largest stone structure in the world; more than 2,000,000 blocks, averaging 2½ tons, were used in its construction. The pyramid was originally 481 feet high, but the removal of part of the apex has reduced its height by 31 feet. Each side stretches 755 feet in length — yet astonishingly enough the corners form almost perfect right angles. The facing stones are fitted so accurately that the joints are all but invisible.

The distinctive feature of the second pyramid is the substantial portion of limestone facing preserved near its apex. Built on higher ground than the Great

Pyramid, Chephren's monument gives the illusion of greater height; in fact, it is slightly smaller and steeper. Originally measuring 471 feet high, its present height is only 447 feet.

The third and smallest pyramid was erected by Mycerinus, Chephren's successor. Its height is 204 feet; when first built, it was fourteen feet higher. Unlike the other two, its lower courses are faced with red granite.

It was not mere size or technical skill that impressed the Greeks and prompted their choice of Wonders. Rather, their selections share one preeminent quality: a grandiose vision. And indeed, the vastness of the pyramids is dwarfed by the metaphysical conceptions that inspired their creation.

The pyramids had been standing for more than two thousand years by the time Nebuchadnezzar built the *Hanging Gardens of Babylon* in the sixth century B.C. According to legend, the king's favorite wife was homesick in flat, rainless Babylon; she yearned for the lush, hilly terrain of her native land. To ease her loneliness, Nebuchadnezzar built the gardens on the palace grounds.

The word "hanging" is a misnomer, the result of faulty translation of a Latin word. The gardens were laid out on a tiered series of balconies or terraces resting on a vaulted foundation. Scholars estimate that the structure rose to a height of nearly four hundred feet.

Thousands of tons of soil were planted with flower beds, vines, and fruit-bearing trees. In specially cooled apartments in the interior of this artificial mountain, the queen and her court could escape the heat of the city.

In the course of excavations at Babylon in 1903, German archaeologist Robert Koldewey uncovered what may have been part of the gardens' massive substructure. Apart from this discovery, no trace remains of the fabulous edifice.

Every four years the city of Olympia in the western Peloponnessus was the site of the Olympic Games; it was also the foremost sanctuary of Zeus, king of the gods. To adorn his temple, the renowned sculptor Phidias created an extraordinary forty-foot-high *Statue of Zeus* in the fifth century B.C. Although the gold and marble figure has disappeared, the glowing testimony of Pausanias, a second-century-A.D. writer, amply justifies its reputation. Seated on an elaborate golden throne encrusted with ivory

and precious stones, Zeus was portrayed with an olive wreath in his hair, golden sandals on his feet, and an ornamental cloak about his shoulders. He held in his right hand an image of Victory; in his left, a scepter supporting an eagle.

The *Temple of Artemis* at Ephesus in Asia Minor also housed a large statue dedicated to a deity — but in this case the Greeks viewed the entire shrine as a Wonder. In the late fourth century B.C. the citizens of Ephesus erected a temple that rivaled the Parthenon at Athens in size and fame. Approximately 400 feet long and 220 feet wide, the marble structure was supported by 127 Ionic columns, each 60 feet high. The

Roman historian Pliny the Elder recorded that the interior overflowed with statuary, paintings, and other treasures.

It has been claimed that this shrine to Artemis, an Asiatic fertility-goddess adopted by the Greeks as their goddess of hunting (and later by the Romans as Diana), attracted more pilgrims than any other building in . the ancient world — until A.D. 262, when invading barbarian Goths destroyed the temple. Even its site was unknown until the mid-nineteenth century, when an English archaeologist unearthed part of its foundation and discovered some sculptural fragments amid the rubble.

In addition to the Olympian Zeus, the Greeks included a second statue among the Wonders of the World. Three times the size of Phidias's masterpiece, the *Colossus of Rhodes* must have been an awe-inspiring sight. To commemorate a hard-won victory over the Macedonian king Demetrius in 305 B.C., the citizens of Rhodes commissioned a statue of their sun-god Helios. The sculptor, Chares of Lindus, supposedly fashioned the bronze figure from weapons left by

the retreating army. The statue was completed in 280 B.C. and was placed high on a jetty overlooking the harbor — not, as a persistent medieval legend would have it, straddling the harbor.

The Colossus was toppled by an earthquake in 224 B.C. and it was never reconstructed. Its fragments were finally carted away in the seventh century A.D. by a junk dealer, who sold the metal for scrap. Not a single piece has survived.

A widow's devotion was the motive force behind the creation of another Wonder in Asia Minor, the *Mausoleum of Halicarnassus*. When Prince Mausolus died in 353 B.C., his wife, Artemisia, determined to honor his memory — and Greek architects, sculptors, and craftsmen were assembled to erect a massive tomb. The complex consisted of a stone platform containing the sarcophagus, thirty-six Ionic columns, and a graceful

stepped pyramid topped by a horse-drawn chariot in which stood colossal marble statues of the prince and his wife. Stone lions flanked the stairs that led to the tomb, which was adorned with sculptural friezes and reliefs.

Severely damaged by earthquakes, the monument was in ruins by the 1500's. In the nineteenth century English excavators recovered so many fragments that they were able to reconstruct its probable appearance. But even if those pieces had not been discovered, Mausolus would be remembered: his name has become a generic term for monumental tombs.

The small fishing village that Alexander the Great chose as his capital in Egypt became, after his death, the cultural center of the Greek world and the site of the seventh Wonder — the *Pharos*

of Alexandria. Soscratus of Cnidus built the enormous lighthouse in the third century B.C., during the reign of Ptolemy II. Constructed entirely of white marble, the Pharos rose in pyramidal stages to a height of four hundred feet. Its base housed an extensive military barracks; its apex, a powerful beacon that could be seen three hundred miles out at sea.

In A.D. 1375 the Pharos was totally destroyed by an earthquake. All that remains are the admiring accounts of travelers to Alexandria who proclaimed the lighthouse a marvel.

Selected Bibliography

Aldred, Cyril. *Akhanaten, Pharaoh of Egypt*. New York: McGraw-Hill, 1968.

Badawy, Alexander. *A History of Egyptian Architecture;* Vol. I, *From the Earliest Times to the End of the Old Kingdom*. Cairo: Giza Studio Misr, 1954.

Bevan, E. R. *The House of Ptolemy: A History of Egypt Under the Ptolemaic Dynasty*. Chicago: Argonaut Publishers, 1968.

Brandon, S. G. F., ed. *Ancient Empires*. New York: Newsweek, 1970.

Carter, Howard. *The Tomb of Tut.Ankh.Amen.*, 3 vols. London: Cassel & Co., Ltd., 1923-33.

Cottrell, Leonard. *Lost Worlds*. New York: American Heritage, 1962.

Davies, Nina M. and Gardiner, Alan H. *Ancient Egyptian Paintings*. Chicago: University of Chicago Press, 1936.

Edwards, I. E. S. *The Pyramids of Egypt*. Harmondsworth: Penguin Books Ltd., 1947.

Egyptian Museum/Cairo. New York: Newsweek, 1969.

Emery, W. B. *Archaic Egypt*. Harmondsworth: Penguin Books Ltd., 1961.

Fakhry, Ahmed. *The Pyramids*. Chicago: University of Chicago Press, 1961.

Forster, E. M. *Alexandria*. New York: Doubleday & Co., Inc., 1961.

Gardiner, Alan H. *Egypt of the Pharaohs*. London: Oxford University Press, 1961.

Hassan, Selim. *The Sphinx: Its History in the Light of Recent Excavations*. London: Oxford University Press, 1949.

Herold, J. Christopher. *Bonaparte in Egypt*. London: H. Hamilton Ltd., 1962.

Kinross, Lord. *Portrait of Egypt*. New York: William Morrow & Co., Inc., 1966.

Lange, K. and Hirmer, M. *Egypt: Architecture, Sculpture, Painting*. London: Phaidon Press Ltd., 1956.

Michalowski, Kazimierz. *Art of Ancient Egypt*. New York: Harry N. Abrams, Inc., 1970.

Montet, Pierre. *Eternal Egypt*. New York: New American Library/World Publishing Co., 1964.

Murray, Margaret A. *The Splendor That Was Egypt*. London: Sidgwick & Jackson Ltd., 1964.

Nims, Charles F. *Thebes of the Pharaohs; Pattern for Everyday Life*. London: Elek Books Ltd., 1965.

Stewart, Desmond. *Cairo: 5500 Years*. New York: Thomas Y. Crowell Co., 1968.

———. *The Middle East: The Temple of Janus*. New York: Doubleday & Co., Inc., 1971.

Wilson, John A. *The Culture of Ancient Egypt*. Chicago: University of Chicago Press, 1951.

Acknowledgments and Picture Credits

The Editors make grateful acknowledgment for the use of excerpted material from the following works:

Caesar and Cleopatra by George Bernard Shaw. Copyright 1962 by the Bernard Shaw Estate. The excerpt appearing on pages 153-56 is reproduced by permission of the Society of Authors for the Bernard Shaw Estate.

Departmental Ditties, Barrack-Room Ballads and Other Verses by Rudyard Kipling. Copyright 1890 by Rudyard Kipling. The excerpt appearing on page 152 is reproduced by permission of Mrs. George Bambridge.

Seventy Years in Archaeology by Flinders Petrie. Copyright 1960 by Flinders Petrie. The excerpt appearing on page 160 is reproduced by permission of BPC Publishing Limited.

The Eastern Key by Abd Al-Latif al-Baghdadi. Translated by Kamal Hafuth Zand and John A. and Ivy E. Videan. Copyright 1965 by the translators. The excerpt appearing on pages 140-42 is reproduced by permission of George Allen & Unwin Limited.

The Editors would like to express their particular appreciation to John G. Ross and to the following individuals and organizations for their assistance in producing this volume:

Sylvia Anderle, New York
The Brooklyn Museum — Richard Fazzini
The Coptic Museum, Cairo — Salib Maher
The Egyptian Museum, Cairo — Henri Riad
Marilyn Flaig, New York
Kate Lewin, Paris
Gamal Moukhtar, Cairo
U.A.R. Tourist Office, New York — Samir Khalil

The title or description of each picture appears after the page number (boldface) followed by its location. Photographic credits appear in parentheses. The following abbreviations are used:

BkM   — The Brooklyn Museum
BrM   — The British Museum
EM,C (JGR) — Egyptian Museum, Cairo (John G. Ross)
MMA   — The Metropolitan Museum of Art

ENDPAPERS Papyrus of the mummy of Hunefer being escorted to the necropolis from *Book of the Dead of Ani,* 19th Dynasty. BrM (Michael Holford) HALF TITLE Symbol designed by Jay J. Smith Studio FRONTISPIECE Painted limestone stele of Chancellor Nefer-yu, 8th Dynasty. MMA, Gift of J. Pierpont Morgan, 1912 **9** Silver reflector from Thebes, 18th Dynasty. MMA, Fletcher Fund, 1920 **10-11** Limestone relief of a funeral procession, 19th Dynasty. BrM (Michael Holford) **12-13** Gray schist head of Userkaf against red granite colossal head of Userkaf from Sakkara, 5th Dynasty. EM,C (JGR)

CHAPTER I **15** Ivory statuette of Cheops from Abydos, 4th Dynasty. EM,C **16-17** From left, the pyramids of Mycerinus, Chephren, and Cheops at Giza (John G. Ross) **18** The Grand Gallery of the Great Pyramid at Giza. The Rosicrucian Society **19** Map by Francis & Shaw **20** Feluccas on the Nile (John G. Ross) **21** left, Painted pottery bird deity from El Ma'mariya, *c.* 4000 B.C.; bottom, Flint and ivory knife of a hunter from Abu Zeidan, *c.* 3200 B.C. Both BkM; top, Two slate palettes from the predynastic era. The Museum of Fine Arts, Boston **22** top and bottom, Both sides of slate Narmer Palette from Hierakonpolis, *c.* 3100 B.C. EM,C (JGR) **23** Limestone stele of King Zet from Abydos, 1st Dynasty. Louvre **24-25** Papyrus of Ta-di-Mut, Singer of Amen, 21st Dynasty. EM,C (JGR) **26** Black diorite statue of Chephren, 4th Dynasty. EM,C (JGR) **27** Dark schist statue of King Mycerinus between the Goddess Hathor and the Goddess of Diospolis Parva, 4th Dynasty. EM,C (JGR) **28** Inscription showing Imhotep's name and that of Zoser. EM,C (JGR) **29** Step Pyramid of Zoser at Sakkara, *c.* 2660 B.C. (John G. Ross)

CHAPTER II **31** Relief of Sesostris I as Osiris and as himself on a pillar from Karnak, 12th Dynasty. EM,C (JGR) **32** Bas-relief of Ptah-hotep from *mastaba* at Sakkara, 5th Dynasty (John G. Ross) **34** left, Statue of Zoser in his *sirdab* to the north of the Step Pyramid at Sakkara, 3rd Dynasty (John G. Ross); right, Faience *ushabtis,* 21st dynasty. EM,C (JGR) **35** Ceramic tiles from Zoser's tomb in the Step Pyramid at Sakkara. EM,C (JGR) **36** The Bent Pyramid at Dahshur (John G. Ross) **38** The three pyramids at Giza (John G. Ross) **39** Close-up detail of Cheop's Great Pyramid at Giza (John G. Ross) **40** Diagram of the Great Pyramid of Giza, from *Histoire de l'Art Egyptien* by Prisse d'Avennes, Paris, 1878 **41** Diagram of a pyramid complex by Francis & Shaw **42** Funerary papyrus showing Egyptian cosmology. EM,C (JGR) **43** Wall painting of Ay as a priest, from Tutankhamen's tomb at Thebes, 18th Dynasty (Michael Holford)

CHAPTER III **45** Scottish troops in front of the Sphinx after the battle of Tell el-Kebir, 1882. Radio Times Hulton Library **46-47** View of Giza. From left, Chephren's pyramid, the Sphinx, and the Great Pyramid (John G. Ross) **48** Black granite sphinx of Amenhemet III, from Tanis, 12th Dynasty. EM,C (JGR) **49** Red granite sphinx of Hashepsowe, 18th Dynasty. EM,C (JGR)

CHAPTER IV **51** Stele of Tuthmosis IV between the paws of the Sphinx of Giza, 18th Dynasty (John G. Ross) **52** Black granite statue of Tuthmosis IV and his mother, Queen Tio, 18th Dynasty. EM,C (JGR) **53** Colossal statue of Amenhotep III and his wife, Tiye, 18th Dynasty. EM,C (JGR) **54** Genealogical chart of 18th Dynasty by Francis & Shaw **55** Black granite statue of the tutor Senmut with Princess Neferura, 18th Dynasty. EM,C (JGR) **56-57** Mortuary temple of Queen Hashepsowe at Deir el-Bahri, 18th Dynasty. Freelance Photographers Guild (Duncan Edwards) **58** Relief of Tuthmosis III and Asiatic prisoners from the Temple of Amen-Re at Karnak, 18th Dynasty. Freelance Photographers Guild (Duncan Edwards) **59** Statue of a Nubian captive, from Sakkara, 18th Dynasty. BkM **61** Detail of schist statue of Tuthmosis III, from Karnak, 18th Dynasty. EM,C (JGR) **62** Heraldic columns of Tuthmosis III at Karnak, 18th Dynasty. The Rosicrucian Society **63** Hypostyle Hall in the Temple of Amen-Re at Karnak, 18th Dynasty. Freelance Photographers Guild (Duncan Edwards) **64** Sandstone statue of Akhenaten, 18th Dynasty. EM,C (JGR) **66** left, Wooden statue of the Sheikh el-Beled, 5th Dynasty; center, Painted limestone statue of the dwarf Seneb and his family, 6th Dynasty; right, Black granite statue of Amenhemet III, 12th Dynasty. All, EM,C (JGR) **67** Quartzite head of Queen Nefertiti, 18th Dynasty. EM,C (JGR) **68** Relief of Nefertiti kissing daughter, 18th Dynasty. BkM **69** Limestone relief of Akhenaten, Nefertiti, and princess worshiping Aten, 18th Dynasty. EM,C (JGR) **70-71** Papyrus of the ceremony of weighing of the souls from the *Book of the Dead of Ani,* 19th Dynasty. BrM. **73** Wooden stele of a worshiper adoring Re-Harakhte, Late Dynastic Period. Louvre (Giraudon)

INDEX